S0-ATW-086

Stuart Library
of Western Americana

UNIVERSITY OF
THE PACIFIC

STOCKTON,
CALIFORNIA

THE AUTHOR OF THIS BOOK

ANTHONY AMARAL

Anthony Amaral was born in Yonkers, New York, in 1930. After his graduation from high school he had become so interested in the lore and history of the Great West that he made the long jump to California to finish his education — enrolling at the California State Polytechnic College, at Pomona, where he graduated with a bachelor's degree in social science.

Before he had finished college he was already absorbed in writing about the historical west, with particular emphasis on the horse and its vital niche in the history of man. His work was soon appearing in many magazines of western and historical flavor. And out of this perceptive and continuing interest came his first full-length book, COMANCHE, a study of the lone horse which survived the Custer Battle.

It is understandable that this interest should lead him into the world of Will James, the gifted and enigmatic cowboy artist and writer. What started out as an article grew into a book, as the riddle of James' life was gradually pierced by research and interviews that took the author over America and Canada.

Anthony Amaral is married, and now lives in Dayton, Nevada. He is a librarian at Carson City. All the research notes, letters, pictures and ephemeral material that have gone into the production of this splendid biography have been given to the special collections library of the University of Nevada.

WILL JAMES
THE GILT EDGED COWBOY

WESTERNLORE GREAT WEST AND INDIAN SERIES

XXXIV

Will James

the Gilt Edged Cowboy

by

ANTHONY AMARAL

WESTERNLORE PRESS . . . 1967 . . . LOS ANGELES 90041

LIBRARY

JUL 1 2 1973

UNIVERSITY OF THE PACIFIC

268164

Western
Americana

PS
3570
J297
A48

COPYRIGHT 1967

BY ANTHONY A. AMARAL

The letter on pages 81 and 82 is reprinted with the permission of Charles Scribner's Sons from *Editor to Author: The Letters of Maxwell E. Perkins*, edited by John Hall Wheelock. Copyright 1950 by Charles Scribner's Sons.

Library of Congress Catalog No. 67-17654

PRINTED IN THE UNITED STATES OF AMERICA BY WESTERNLORE PRESS

"A boy's will is the wind's will,
  And the thoughts of youth are long, long thoughts."

OLD LAPLAND SONG.

Illustrations

Introduction

FOUR YEARS AGO, when the idea for a story on Will James came to
to this writer's mind, the thought carried no more than an article
length survey. It would relate the events following the last chapter of James' autobiography, *Lone Cowboy,* and would span
about ten years; from 1930 when *Lone Cowboy* was published, to
1942, the year James died.

Background was of course necessary, and *Lone Cowboy* the
logical reference. As a boy I had read this minor classic and
could still recall an undeniable thrill from the adventures James
related. Even as I searched the book again, and now with a perspective lengthened from boyhood to maturity, it still conjured a
unique, venturesome tale; vivid in content and expressed with
the momentum and full-flavored jargon of the westerner. James
spreads a self-portrait that easily imparts versimilitude to his
reader.

Lone Cowboy begins near the turn of the century, with the
pathos of a little boy, Will James, orphaned in the great Montana
range country. His parents were moving toilsomely by wagon
from Texas to Canada, when in June, 1892, James is born "close
to the sod," near the Judith Basin in Montana. "If I could have
seen far enough," says James, "I could have glimpsed ponies
through the flap of the tent on my first day while listening to the
bellowing of cattle and the ringing of my dad's spurs."

James does not remember his mother, a Californian of Spanish and Irish-Scotch descent, as she dies shortly after James is born. Her maiden name was Rodriguez, which James claims as the origin of his middle name, Roderick.

James' father, born and raised in West Texas, and a cattle drover during the *eighties*, is killed by a maddened steer when James is about four years old.

To a friend of James' father, a French trapper named Jean Beaupre, James is entrusted. Together they travel the wilderness trails north into the Peace River country of Canada and along the Mackenzie, setting trap lines and living at isolated camps. James is practically a child of nature, and nature teaches her own the lure and lore of her ways. He learns that when the geese fly north in the spring he and Bopy, as he calls his guardian, will abandon their snowshoes. They will take to saddle and pack horses, ride south over mountain passes and through valleys into the United States and the cow country for which James feels a strong affinity. And when the geese herald their southward course, the boy senses that he and Bopy must ride north and again exchange their saddles for snowshoes and settle to a winter of trap laying.

Education?

Catalogues, old newspapers and magazines picked up at the ranches or found in abandoned cabins afford James the only hints of other ways of life. For Bopy is a wanted man, and shuns civilization. Still, the wilderness patriarch informally teaches the boy to read French. And, with greater exactness, James is taught the ways of living off the land and on the land — covering a fire with grass and causing a smoke smudge to keep away the mosquitoes because, Bopy tells him, "if you kill one the others get peeved and pick it out on you."

When Bopy takes to the course of his trap lines, James must rustle and amuse himself in a line shack as he awaits Bopy's return. He has a horse to ride, but shortly tires of the geographical limits sternly ordered by Bopy. While still very young, James feels the urge to draw, and uses charcoal from the fire to express with natural aptitude the forms of wild animals. But his favorite theme is cowboys and their horses. Drawing urges him unremittingly in those lonely days and Bopy, recognizing the boy's pleasure, gives him pencils and pads of paper as New Year's gifts.

Often alone, restless and inquisitive, unusual events fill his spacious vacuum. James tells the story of when he adopts two wolves, *Gros* and *Otay* as pets. He remembers shooting his first bear with Bopy's muzzle loader when he was about ten. Then there is the year of agony while his stomach heals from burns after drinking a can of lye.

These are the wilds and the dangers of his life as a youthful Nimrod. And yet he never fails to tell about the beauty of the country, or the drifting back and forth with the seasons over the great western landscape when it was still primeval and still challenging.

When James is about fourteen, personal tragedy searches him out again. Early one morning he finds Bopy missing. He searches for him, but finds only Bopy's water bucket that the thawing current is battering against a river bank. He has a premonitory feeling.

For days he rides his horse up and down the river, calling and searching for Bopy. Finally, his mind becomes resigned to his feeling that Bopy has drowned.

James takes the horses and, continuing the pattern he has learned, rides to the cow country. He is completely independent now, alone, but seemingly never lonely. Now comes the stories of life in the cow camps, on bucking horses, chasing mustangs and contesting in rodeos. He is a tramp cowboy with a pack horse, and an unrelenting urge to drift. James rides from the cow country of the north to the cow country of the south; from Canada to Mexico.

"If you follow my trail," he says, "it'll look as though a centipede had dipped his legs in ink and then just sorta paraded on that map for a spell."

Finally one rough bronc proves to James that he is no longer a saddle athlete, and he turns to his other loves, art and writing. There is the struggle for recognition, but he claims that victory, and grows tall to the public in personifying the real cowboy. Critics give a warm appraisal of his writing and art by acclaiming them an authentic touch of a way of life that western fiction has cranked out of reality. James, reports one book reviewer, is ". . . no lily-fingered, typewriter-tapping dude with the background of a two-week visit to Santa Fe . . ."[1]

He is *the* cowboy artist and writer, a charming exotic who knows the smell of sage, the pungent sweat odor of cow-work, and the freakish twists of a sunfishing bronc. In many ways James emerges like Owen Wister's *The Virginian,* a cowpuncher who has roamed the west from the arid southwest to the verdant northwest, spurred by his "untamed soul." Both are heroes in their own right, the Virginian through a sense of righteousness, and James as an honest chronicler of the real west. And also like Wister's *The Virginian,* James' *Lone Cowboy* is mostly fiction.

The preceding was not known to this writer at the time when an article survey about Will James was the primary thought. Once known, however, and since only very few others knew of James' subterfuge, this book became the outgrowth. Consequently, James' life became a fascinating pursuit, but frustrating to piece together coherently. He left no intensely personal record of his real life. What he has written reflects a boyhood fantasy tempered with some reality into a truth and beauty as he saw

[1]"Our Family Album," *Ladies' Home Journal,* Nov., 1927.

them. And as will be seen, James contrived to hide his personal identity even after his death.

Most of James' books are conspicuously lacking in names, dates and places. *Lone Cowboy* is the most notable. He excuses these omissions (possibly with a bit a shrewdness) in his preface to *Lone Cowboy*:

> "Here's a long story for you with no names in it to speak of . . . so you won't be bothered by the names of the creeks and the cow camps you might never heard of . . . and of riders you wouldn't know . . ."

J. Frank Dobie was not convinced. In his *Life and Literature of the Southwest,* he writes skeptically about *Lone Cowboy* being "without a date or a geographical location less generalized than the space between Canada and Mexico."

Ross Santee, the more polished contemporary of James, wrote this author of his annoyance with James when he would talk about the "southern countries" that he had worked. One time Santee remarked to James, "Goddamn it, states have names, an' when a cowboy works for an outfit the brand is known."

It is interesting, in light of the above, that those who knew James had mixed opinions about him. While they consider him to have been a first class cowboy and a congenial friend, they also agree that he was either shy or sly when it came to talking about himself in specific terms. Ross Santee speaks of this habit in James as, *muy coyote,* the quiet sort who is noncommittal about his past. Certainly this in itself is no complete character trait. In those days one spoke stingily about himself, and asked even less about another man's past. James, however, was silent to the point of taciturnity which shaded into furtive suspicion.

But for thousands of other readers of *Lone Cowboy* there were no doubts as to what James wrote and described as his life being essentially true. Only by a quirk, during this biographical research, did this writer overturn a stone that logically should not have attracted attention. In sequence it led to other stone-turning until another Will James was revealed. Every success is supposed to have its private hell. This hidden Will James became the hell of the one in *Lone Cowboy*. Not even James' wife was to know of the Mr. Hyde complex of her husband during his lifetime.

There is no author's intent of careening toward sensationalism by debunking Will James. And, in the matter of extremes, neither will he be idealized as an honest Oracle out of the west (as he has been) at a time when myths of the west were the fashion. Either approach to a biography is bound to miss the essential meaning and volatile shadings of a life.

In view of this new evaluation of Will James, *Lone Cowboy*, which is a minor classic, will be somewhat desecrated — and with it, a myth of a man and his works. But since man is prone to offer harsh judgments before spading the facts deeply, maybe it is fitting if a thought of James' is considered first:

"To my way of thinking anybody with a lot of nerve is never real bad all the way ..."

— ANTHONY A. AMARAL.

Dayton, Nevada
February, 1967

WILL JAMES
THE GILT EDGED COWBOY

Chapter One

OASIS, UTAH, in the fall of 1914, wasn't much more than what its name implies. With only a railroad-born array of weather-dried shipping pens, a small hotel, barber shop and a few homes, Oasis was nonetheless a welcome relief from the monotonous stretch of desert, dry lakes and drab mountain chains for anyone driving cattle from eastern Nevada. Ely, Nevada was also a shipping point, and the logical terminal for cattle in that part of the state. Stock raisers drove their cattle to Ely. Rustlers sneaked them into Oasis.

In the barber shop of that desert town, a saddle-fatigued rider sat slumped in the barber chair. While taking a bath in a tin tub in the back room he had fallen asleep until the barber awakened him. Now he was dozing again while his face was being shaved.

His name at this time was Will James, a skinny, poorly dressed, twenty-two year old rider and bronc buster. He was known throughout Nevada cow country and, if not by name, then by reputation as the cowpuncher who drew pictures of bucking horses which sometimes covered entire walls of ranch and bunk houses. Local ranchers had another name for this kind — boomer — a drifter from one outfit to another, working when he needed money, and pursuing his own pleasures and interests when he had a few dollars of his own.

Bronc busting was his specialized calling. He prided himself as being one of the best in that hazardous trade, and knew that he was looked up to by other riders because his horses were never spoiled or broken in spirit. No one had ever called him a *bronc fighter*, a derogative term for a *buster* of little talent. But soon, he would be called a cattle rustler.

About twenty days before, James and another boomer of dubious reputation, named Lew Hackberry (now using the *alias* Harry Bradberry), were working at the Jim Riordan Ranch in Nye County, Nevada, when they decided to quit and drift southward. In the white sage country called Spring Valley (near the White Pine and Lincoln County lines), they came upon thirty-one head of heifers and cows belonging to the Swallow Brothers' ranch at Shoshone. The cattle had wandered farther south than usual, and to the quick eye of Hackberry or James, no horse tracks showed to indicate that Swallow Brothers' riders were aware that these cattle had drifted. In an apparently easy manner, the two riders decided to drive the cattle into Utah, ship them from Oasis and sell them in Denver.

During the remainder of that day they rested themselves and their horses. At the first hint of dusk they started the stock moving southeasterly. The two boomers drove only at night, and hid themselves and the stock in the hills during the day. Their circuitous route took them two hundred miles in a northeasterly direction, across the Utah line, and through desert and hill country that was out of the way of traveled routes. Nights were cold, and snow had blinded their way several times. Little sleep was taken by either man during their clandestine ten-day drive. On the ninth night they drove the cows up from Antelope Springs along the eastern edge of the Cricket Mountains in Utah. On the final night James let the cattle bed down a few miles outside of Oasis while Hackberry rode into town and engaged a railroad car to move the cows into Denver, where they were consigned in Hackberry's name. Between ten and eleven that night, James drove the footsore cows into the stockyards adjacent to the railroad siding. Near midnight, they were loaded into the stock cars and, accompanied by Hackberry, on their way to Denver. James was to sell the horses the next morning and purchase a ticket to Provo, Utah, where he would meet Hackberry and claim his share for the sale of the cows.

While James dozed in the barber chair early that next morning, a friend of one of the Swallow brothers heard about some cattle with the Lazy GS brand having been shipped the night before. That was unusual. He followed a hunch, and sent a wire to the Swallow brothers' father in Salt Lake who immediately wired the news to his sons in Shoshone.

A couple of men strolled into the barber shop while James was being shaved. James was half-asleep when he heard one of the men telling the barber about some cattle having been shipped the past evening and of some suspicion as to the bona-fide owner.

As soon as James left the barber chair he cancelled his trip to Provo, collected the two horses from the livery, and rode toward Fillmore, southeast of Oasis.

Meanwhile, Richard Swallow and some of his riders were gathering strays out of the mountains in the Connors Pass country when he was notified by a rider sent by Mrs. Swallow that some of their cattle had appeared in Oasis. White Pine County Sheriff, C. S. Crain, had also been notified. It required two days to make certain that the cattle were missing, and afterwards Crain sent a telegram to the constable in Denver, notifying him that stolen cattle were in Denver, and to apprehend a Harry Bradberry on suspicion of theft. The Denver sheriff wired back that a Harry Bradely *(sic)* had sold a car of cattle in Denver for

$1,471.60, and had paid his bill at the Albany Hotel.[1] There was no other trace of the man.

James, however, was apprehended by Sheriff Dougherty of Fillmore. As James and Hackberry were, according to the *Ely Record*[2] "... well known throughout this section...," Sheriff Crain put a tracer on James, since he had ridden away from the Riordan Ranch with Hackberry and both had disappeared at the same time as the cattle.

In *Lone Cowboy*,[3] James tells of stealing the cattle, but has doctored the facts and promoted some fiction. Instead of being an opportunist with regard to some strayed cattle, he is instead on a revenge compulsion. A "home guard" (cowman who never left his part of the country) accuses James of purposely killing a bronc because James was not able to ride the horse. James argues that the horse is one of the "crookedest outlaws in the country," and the kind that would throw himself over backwards. On the last ride James makes with the bronc, the horse does just that, and breaks its neck.

Adding to James' resentment of the home guard crew, he gets into a fight with the one who accused him of killing the horse. Just as James is "getting in a few licks," some of the crew get a hold on James from behind, and clamp his arms down.

"The worst part for me," says James, "was that nobody got holt of the home guard and he took advantage of that to do some pounding."

After the beating, James is intent on settling the score. Stealing that outfit's cattle and making "them hunt the country" for their stock seems a just reprisal. James drives the cattle to a shipping point and, to get the cattle into the holding pen, he has to take down part of the fence. But in replacing it, he inadvert-

---

[1]*Ely Record*, Nov. 24, 1914.
[2]*Ibid.*
[3]*Lone Cowboy*, p. 299-336.

ently sets a post upside down. The next morning, suspicion is aroused because of the upside down post and James, being a stranger in town, is suspected and caught. James' most interesting line about this incident in *Lone Cowboy* is when he thinks of possibly escaping by using a pistol hidden in his boot. (James did carry a pistol in his boot for many years, even after he was married.) But instead, he writes, "I decided to stay and take a chance on clearing the name I was then using." Of course, James was using the name, Will James.

James was apprehended about the middle of November, 1914, and taken to the county jail at Ely. He admitted assisting Hackberry in the theft and that Hackberry had all the money. James was held in jail for two months before a formal complaint was drawn, and a warrant issued. This excessive length of time was from the anticipation of apprehending Hackberry, for whom a $100 reward was posted on December 14.

Finally, on January 25, 1915, James was brought into Justice Court for preliminary examination. He entered a plea of not guilty through his counsel, J. M. Lockhart. Richard Swallow testified for the State.

Lockhart made an effort to shift the bulk of the stealing initiative onto Hackberry, and also attempted to build a case about the cattle running wild. The court was not impressed, especially since the cattle bore brands and earmarks. Richard Swallow testified that in a conversation with James, while the latter was in jail, James admitted that stealing the cattle seemed "a way to get some easy money."[4] James was held over on $2,000 bail, and his trial scheduled for early spring. He could not put up the bail, and no one volunteered the bond.

With his easy manner, James made friends with jail officials during his confinement. From them James requested paper and

[4]Reporter's Transcript; State of Nevada *vs.* Will R. James, White Pine County, Nevada, 1915.

pencil, and he would sketch for hours. He gave his drawings to those who asked for them. Many were impressed by his art, as reported by the local newspapers:

SOMETHING OF AN ARTIST

Will James . . . has made many friends among county officials and others. He is a natural artist and since confinement in jail has had time to devote to drawing. His work is especially good on ranch scenes, and with proper training he would soon be able to do first class work. His confession was secured by District Attorney Jurich, who, however, made no promises as to clemency on the part of the court.[5]

Three days before James was to go to trial, he changed his plea to guilty. On April 27, he was found guilty of grand larceny, and sentenced to the Nevada State Prison at Carson City for a term of twelve to fifteen months.[6]

[5]*Ely Record,* April 30, 1915.
[6]*Ibid.*

Chapter Two

NEVADA HAD ITS PRISON in the confines of what was previously the Warm Springs Stage Station, about two miles east of Carson City. From his cell, James could see sagebrush land spreading to brown foothills and then to the Sierra Nevada Mountains.

He had only a few visitors while confined. Mary Riordan, at whose husband's ranch James had worked, visited once while trading in Carson City. Mrs. Riordan was fond of James, since he often helped her wash dishes at the ranch, and did other small considerations which had pleased her. James would leave her pictures he had drawn of ranch scenes and a dance which was held at the Riordan ranch.

When she visited James, she brought him pencils and drawing pads.

"Now I know what a mustang feels like when corralled," was his first, but humorously uttered comment to her. They talked about half an hour. Nothing was mentioned about the cattle incident. Mostly, James talked about art. He told her he was becoming mighty conscious about the natural life zones of desert, hills and mountains, and had been studying them from his window. "Light," he told her, "changes the moods and the land color every time the sun moves."

The prison policy then, as now, encouraged its inmates to take up hobbies. Some of the ranch hands braided rawhide quirts, bosals and saddles.

"All I knowed was riding," reflected James, "and that outfit [the prison] sure didn't care for me to do any riding, so I was put to one job after another."

James' first duty was serving as *flunky* in the mess hall, then as wood chopper, and later, as a trusty, he waited on the guards' tables. Shortly after he became a trusty he tangled in an argument with a cook, and was sent back to chopping wood.

Most likely, James wouldn't have been in prison at that moment if he had gone along with Curly Eagles, Skeeter Bill and Jim Campbell. James met Curly and Skeeter in Ogden, Utah a few months before he went on the cattle caper. Curly and Skeeter had come down from Pendleton with bucking stock, and had hopes of promoting a bronc show in Ogden. But they went broke in two days and decided to head for Nevada. They sold their few horses and hocked their saddles for train fare and some spending money.

"We were dealing with the shop owner," recounts Curly, "and were aware of this other cowboy sort of eye-feasting about the place. Didn't mean much to us; he was kind of like the rest of us, scroungy looking, big hat on his head... Finally after getting some money for our saddles, this other cowboy comes over to us and introduces hisself and says his name's Bill James. We bought a jug and drank and talked."

"Where ya headed?" Bill says.

"We told him we planned catchin' some mustangs around Ely, and Bill said he thought he'd head for that part of the country, too. He told us he had a friend, Jim Campbell, south of Ely, who was running wild horses and that we could join him if we liked. It sounded okay to Skeeter and me, and so we hopped a cattle car going to Ely."

Curly, Skeeter and James teamed with Campbell, but Campbell soon demurred that he had only his own saddle and none to offer his mustanging partners.

"We improvised," said Curly. "Got some collar pads and put a surcingle around and then tied cinch rings to the sides for stirrups."

"We didn't do too well catchin' horses, however. Got a few head, but not enough to make some money on. Finally Bill got disgusted and decides to pull out and head for where he came from. We didn't know where he meant and didn't ask. He took one of the horses he'd broke and we say *adios*.

"The rest of us stays on and soon we start hitting a couple of good catches. We have a bunch together in a few weeks and after some gentling we decided to take them to Hinkley, Utah (a few miles north of Oasis) where we could fatten them before selling.

"We were around Hinkley about three weeks when one morning while checking the stock we noticed three head are missing and figgered they must have headed back toward Nevada. They headed south, then west, and that was the route we followed.

"We camped out, of course, and a little after dark one night, we hear cattle being moved. They're bawlin' and we can also hear some yellin' by a couple of riders. Well, this part of the country has always been sort of a corridor for stolen stock being pushed into Utah. It's queer all right, but none of our business.

"We caught our horses a couple of days later and head them back to Hinkley. It is there that we hear about Bill having pushed some stolen cattle through this country to Oasis a week or so before. I knew then it was Bill and that other jasper, that Skeeter and me heard that night.

"Bill was a good hand with a horse. Like a lot of us though he tied the right stirrup to the saddle if he knew a horse was going to buck bad. Wiry fella. Saw him a couple of times later, in Hollywood, after his success."

Soaking up time in prison wasn't particularly disturbing to James. As long as he had a pencil and paper, or someone to listen to him tell stories, James felt little discomfort while confined. During the last few months of his term, and after he had become something of a favorite to some of the guards, he became a trusty outside the walls and did some horse work with the prison stock.

James was paroled on April 11, 1916, one month earlier than the scheduled end of his sentence. He stayed in Carson City for a few days and heard, through a local bartender, that a rancher from Smith Valley was in town looking for some help. James searched out the rancher, Bill Dressler of the Plymouth Land and Stock Company, but was forewarned by Dressler that the job wasn't riding. What Dressler needed was a milker.

"Can you milk?" Dressler asked.

"Sure," answered James.

James wasn't playing square. He knew nothing about milking, and deemed working for any outfit that drank milk or "pumped" cows, as bad as being a sheepherder. But he was broke, although ten dollars in "gate money," as he called it, was due him from the prison.

At Smith Valley he was assigned twenty-five milk cows that had to be milked twice a day.

"Christ!" recalls Jeff Rice. "He didn't know anything about milking a cow. After two days his hands began to swell."

Jeff had met James once before, around Great Falls, Montana. Both of them were then about eighteen years old, drifting and riding the bronc string. While together in the same part of the country, "we split a bottle between us until we went our separate ways."

Jeff had choked down a laugh when James told him he would be milking the cows. James caught Jeff's smile and said, "I can't blame ya, Jeff. I might as well de-horn my boots."

James had milked the cows twice a day for two weeks when a rider from the Rickey outfit out of Bridgeport, California, stopped by. James asked if any riding jobs were available, and was told there were some broncs needing a rider, if he were interested. James collected what pay was due him and proceeded to Bridgeport.

The broncs were corralled at a line camp near Topaz, the winter range for the Rickey Ranch. They were a husky bunch that had been caught in Nevada, and, for about two weeks, James rode and gentled six of the broncs. Another, a mature stallion, fought stubbornly, and had to be thrown to have a hackamore placed on his head. While another rider was helping to tie down the stallion, the bronc lashed out with a rear leg and caught James in the jaw, knocking him out immediately. His teeth had been in bad condition, and the blow from the stud's hoof loosened and split most of them on the left side of his jaw.

James laid up for a few days, but the pain did not subside. Most of the riders told him he would have to see a dentist, and that thought was inevitable, even to James, who disliked any sort of doctor. He had little money, but knew he could not wait any longer. James turned in his time, and decided to go to Los Angeles.

A few days before he scheduled himself to leave, a rider with a pack horse trailing behind came to the ranch to spend the night. He was Fred Conradt of Reno, another horse breaker with whom James had occasionally ridden in Nevada. Fred tried to persuade James to come with him to Reno. James declined, since he doubted Reno could offer the needed specialist. Fred bolstered his proposal. Since he was going home to see his family and do some local rodeoing, he offered James a free roost while being treated by the dentist. James liked the idea, but still insisted that Los Angeles was the best place for him to go. Before Fred rode out of camp the next morning, he told James to look him up whenever he passed through Reno. "Got some sisters full a'hell," he added.

In Los Angeles James took a room at a small hotel while he scouted for a dentist he could afford. He found one, located near the section that was called Edendale. He also found the Jones Stable, "a little cow country" which supplied horses, buggies, wagons, oxen and stuntmen for the fledgling motion picture industry. James lingered around the stable daily, and made acquaintances. In a short time he was riding and stunting pell-mell in front of the cameras. James has related his early Hollywood days in both *Lone Cowboy* and *Drifting Cowboy*, with varying accounts. But he does make an interesting story about doubling for cowboy stars, jumping horses off twenty-foot cliffs, throwing horses over backwards in the eye of the camera — and "meeting all those show girls — some nice ones, too, of all styles from running to draft types . . ."

Most of the cowboys at the Jones Stable were refugees from the range, enticed to come to Hollywood to lend authenticity to the westerns which were giving the mute cameras something to say in action films. Hollywood was still an unorganized and not fully awake industry, and any cowboy that could ride a horse could earn five dollars a day just galloping a horse, and possibly a twenty-dollar bonus if he pulled a stunt with a horse that satisfied the director. The cowboy riders and stuntmen were clannish, and as rough and hard drinking a bunch of cowboys as has ever assembled anywhere. The Jones Stable was their headquarters, and here they waited for calls from the studios. Jones, however, wasn't running any free rent hangout for the cowboys. He kept them working at building wagons, repairing harness, cleaning tack, and breaking horses while they waited for studio work calls.

"That James kid," remembers Clarence Jones, "was the laziest of the bunch, unless he was on top of a horse. One reason I remember him, and hundreds of cowboys have floated through here in the past fifty years, was because of his drawings. For a while they were tacked all over the place. I only have one now, dated 1916. After James left here, his pictures began to disappear from the barns and sleeping quarters, so I grabbed the one I considered his best."

Jones saw James one more time, about fifteen years later, when James came to the stable to see Rex, the star horse of the Jones string who was to act the title role in the movie version of James' *Smoky*.

James worked for the Thomas Ince Studios, which produced many western pictures, and goes into considerable detail about his doubling and stunting for "that doggoned pink leading man in Six Guns and Rope."[7] The director, according to James, liked his appearance and apparently there might have been a future for him as a western cinema hero. But at the moment, with a few dollars in his pocket, his dental work finished, and the rainy season quieting the cameras and the acting work, James was becoming anxious for the cow country. There, the snow patches were trickling to an end, and the grass shoots spreading patches of green. "Little white faces were coming into the world, and remudas were being run in from winter range in preparation for the spring round-up." Nostalgia was stirring James.

He took the train to Tonopah, Nevada. On and off since about 1910, James had worked for most of the cattle ranches in the Tonopah area. In fact the few outfits that James does describe, by name or brand, in his first stories, center in the Tonopah and eastern Nevada country. Occasionally, when riding jobs were as scarce as his finances, he would work as a mucker in the Goldfield mines.

With a horse under him, James rode toward the Stone Cabin Valley, east of Tonopah, where local ranches converged for combined efforts during the spring and fall round-ups. The Sals-

[7]This motion picture title is not listed in the Catalog of Copyright Entries for Motion Pictures, 1912-39. James' penchant for varnishing certain tales of his is a characteristic of his writing. One can almost, after enough exposure to his work, learn when to take the facts and when to dismiss the elaboration.

bury outfit provided James a job and for two months he worked at the chores of herding strays from out of the Monitor Forest Range and down to the desert "cutting grounds" for branding and castrating.

About June, James quit and decided to drift north. At the Barley Creek Ranch in the Monitor Valley, owned by Joseph Nay, James was invited to stay the night. He put his saddle and pack horse into a corral and helped Joe Nay butcher hogs. James stayed ten days through encouragement of the Nay family, who immediately liked his subtle humor and his stories about Hollywood.

Olephia Nay[8] was thirteen at the time, and remembers James vividly, since she also had an interest in art. In the evening she and James would sketch, and James would advise her about anatomy and positions of horses while bucking and running.

Joe Nay thought James was loco to be just a rider when he could become an artist and "pack in better wages." James mentioned that he would like to be an artist, "like that one [Charlie Russell] in Montana." This was a wish that James had frequently made to himself, but he took his art thoughts more seriously in times of depression and discouragement, than in times when all was going well for him. He was still young and liked to drift, "to see the country." Traipsing was easy-going, and if he had money and a couple of horses, his mind eased to the lackadaisical attitude he preferred. The desire to be an artist was within him, but he wasn't so moved as yet to fight for its full-time devotion.

James mounted his horse, left the Nay Ranch, and rode along the now forgotten stock trails to Beowawe in the cattle country around Elko. This part of northern Nevada was a favorite for James. A vast open country where cattle mingled with antelope, it had more than vestiges of the open range days, and was

[8]Now Mrs. Emerson King.

in fact, one of the last few pockets of the range country that still had no branding corrals or chutes, or fences cutting across the land. In his letters to Olephia (James promised that he would comment and "check over" her drawings if she would send them to him) he had said that he would stay in Beowawe. However, he apparently sold his horses and continued north by train until he arrived in Malta, in northeastern Montana. A job was available at the Circle Dot Ranch, winter-feeding cows and breaking a few broncs. James remained there the entire winter.

In the spring, with a good part of his pay saved from his virtual hibernation the winter before, he went south to Tuscarora, about 70 miles north of Elko. For three months he worked on the Old Spanish Ranch. In July, James decided to work another winter in Montana. He sold his horses and started north, going first, however, to Calgary, Canada.

Lloyd Garrison, a Canadian cowpuncher, was home on leave in August, from the Canadian Army. At Calgary, he joined with some of the boys, among whom was James. Garrison had met him once before, around 1914, in Medicine Hat, and believed James had come up from Malta over the wild horse trail.

James told Garrison at this second meeting that things were going bad for him, and that he was going back over the line to join the army. Garrison goes on to say:

"Well, after Bill left, I got with Bob Stadley, Calgary Red, Sleepy Eperson and we were going to make a few of the shows or stampedes. We were traveling in Red's old Model T Ford. First show we hit was at Taber and we run into Bill. So right now he comes with us. I recall he drew bucking horses and cowboys all over the Ford, with colored crayons. So we sure had a lot of admirers in town. We made the Taber show — Bill put on a good ride — Moose Jaw, the Big Gap out of Hardisty, back to Winnifred then to Medicine Hat. All this before I reported back to the army. I recall the last night in Medicine Hat, when we put on a show in the street, Calgary Red did some rope spinning and Bill did the announcin'. We all did a lot of singin' and we all drank too much."

Garrison left the next morning and the rest of the cowboys broke up shortly afterward.

James was out of sight that winter and possibly did return to the Montana country to punch cows from a hay wagon as he did the past winter. By spring of 1918, however, he was in serious trouble with the draft board, who could not locate him. Letters had followed him, but he always was ahead of them. In early May, James rode into Winnemucca, Nevada, to check at the local draft board about his status. They told him that he was about to be sought throughout the country as a draft-dodger. On May 20, 1918 he was inducted, and assigned to Headquarters Company, 21st Infantry and sent to Camp Kearny, California. Less than a year later, in February, James was honorably discharged, with a rank of private.

Chapter Three

SOMETIME between 1917 and 1919 James purposely went to Great Falls, Montana to see the artist, Charlie Russell. Typically, James does not mention Russell by name in *Lone Cowboy*, but refers to him as ". . . that artist which all the cowboys all knowed or heard of . . . I'd been packing some postcards which had been printed from his work . . ."

It may have been one of James' depressed moods that spurred him to see Russell; to hopefully get an evaluation of his own art work from one who "was making a lot of money at that game."

In his free-roaming days, James was always cocky about his talents, which is usually a mate to youthful naiveté. His self-esteem as a cowboy and an artist were in this order of ability, and it would be some years to come before he would realize that art, like living, is best when it is simple, and both are hard to achieve. His only critics had been cowboys and other well meaning encouragers whose opinions were hardly those of experts. James' sketches at this time were cumbersome with details that distracted from the main action, and his horses were depicted in exaggerated "wild west" poses. He still had some learning to do.

When James came to the Russell house, he felt that he had arrived as an artist; that Russell would recognize his talent and provide the ropes for James to hoist himself to fame. Nancy Russell answered the door knock and invited James to sit in the parlor while she went to the studio to announce James. A minute later she returned and escorted James to the studio.

Of Russell, James wrote: "... the whole map of the cow country was on his face. I could see at a glance that he'd squinted over many herds of cattle and that he was all cowboy as well as artist..."[1]

What James didn't expect was the curt and hollow encouragement he received from Russell.

Russell was painting when James silently walked into the studio filled with canvases, smells of oil, and all sorts of western artifacts hanging over chairs and from wall pegs. James stood there for a few minutes, feeling like an awkward intruder. In a corner by himself was Joe DeYong, an artist and protégé of Russell's. (The Russells would gladly have adopted Joe DeYong as a youth but, according to Austin Russell, a nephew, Joe had "a couple of practicing parents of his own who seemed quite fond of him...")[2]

Russell looked up at James, uttered a salutation in the form of a grunt, and focused his attentions back to the canvas in front of him. The painting had bogged him down and he sat in one of his deeply absorbed moods, lost almost completely from anything and anybody around him. It was an engrossment that only a few, as Nancy and Joe, understood in Russell.

James asked Russell about his problem with the painting to crack the impersonal air. Russell mumbled an answer. Annoyed, James held out a batch of his drawings, which Russell took with an outstretched hand without looking at James. Russell laid them on his lap and continued working on his picture. Finally he put his paint brush down, and then shuffled through James' drawings ... "as if they was cards, getting ready to play stud poker and deal out a hand, and just as quick as he shuffled 'em and

[1]*Lone Cowboy,* p. 283.
[2]Austin Russell, *C. M. R., Charles M. Russell, Cowboy Artist,* p. 206.

while I was waiting for surprised remarks, my deck of drawings was handed back to me, and he went to work on his picture again, just as though I still wasn't around and like he'd never seen them pictures of mine . . ."[3]

James asked Russell what he thought of them.

"Good." Russell answered reticently.

James then asked where he could sell them. Russell told him to scatter them around saloons . . . "Somebody might buy them."

James said a polite goodbye, and left.

"I sensed," related Joe DeYong, "that Bill assumed he received something in the nature of a brush-off and I followed him outside to explain the matter. However, his drawing and description of the meeting in *Lone Cowboy* indicated that he still believed that Charlie's attitude was a matter of personal indifference."

Russell's somewhat impersonal attitude paled James' enthusiasm. But it was only a shadow of discouragement, and was soon eclipsed by the memory of the craftsmanship James had seen in Russell's canvases. It only made James' urge to paint more insatiable. He began to realize, as he admitted in later years, that the visit to the Russell studio made him conscious that his own work was only mediocre, and that even natural talent needed practice and study. He longed for a studio of his own, where he could paint, somewhere in the hills and close to the land.

It was in May, 1919 when James came to Reno to visit with Fred Conradt. He found Fred and another cowboy friend named Elmer Freel. Reno became the last location in James' gypsy-ramblings over the west. Here he found a close kinship with Fred and Elmer, and together they became a fun-loving, rowdy and semi-lazy trio. They called themselves the one-elevens (111) and made a pact that whoever of the three would someday own a ranch, would share it with the other two.[4] They

---

[3]*Lone Cowboy,* pp. 285-286.

[4]On James' early illustrations, under his signature, he affixed the colophon, *111,* as his faith in the bond.

broke horses together, entered bronc contests held at the out-
lying ranches and were generally inseparable. Most of the time
they were broke, although James was able to make one to five
dollars now and then sketching advertising posters for local mer-
chants. He was paid $20 by fairground officials to illustrate
posters and a souvenir program for the First Annual Nevada
Round-Up Rodeo held in Reno, July, 1920.

When James first came to Reno, he slept in the alfalfa fields
and later in a stall at the fairgrounds. Fred sneaked James'
clothes in with his own laundry, which his sisters washed. They
became wise to the stunt, but said nothing, since James had
become well liked by Fred's mother.

Fred's family consisted of his parents, four other brothers, and
seven sisters. To Alice, the third youngest, James took an immediate liking. Alice was then about 15, a tall, attractive blonde,
but who couldn't care less about a cowboy. Her parents were
Edward and Mary, who had emigrated from Germany to Hawaii,
where her father felt he could find use for his building trade. But
Hawaii was still developing too slowly, and so the father moved
his family to Oklahoma, where they stayed for only a short time.
Their next move was again temporary, to San Francisco, and
then to Sacramento where he was able to develop a business in
a sawmill. Alice was born in Sacramento in 1904. When she was
about three, her family moved to Reno permanently.

James ate with the Conradts frequently. He told stories of his
life as an orphan, and his tramping all around the country. James
would often direct his comments to Alice, but she would ignore
his attentions. To her, James wasn't much different from most
cowboys, the shiftless sort, and another of Fred's buddies who
seemed all quite the same and without any ambitions. While
Alice was willing to be impersonal to James, her father took an
immediate dislike to him. James was too rowdy to suit the father

and, what was more, he told Alice, James seemed the type that would "have a record."

Although James had poured out his desires to the Conradts of someday being an artist, he still wasted too much time as a fun-lover. Spasmodically, he had spells of studying magazine illus-trations, sketching horses out in the pastures, or studying animal anatomy books. The spells would last a week or two until Fred or Elmer suggested some adventure to pursue, usually a bronc contest. Yet, even the momentary serious pursuits were showing James that he had a style of his own, and that it came to a high polish with even a short time of thoughtful study. James was nearing the time now when a critic would exclaim that James' horses looked as though "they were jumping right out of the page."

If James was too much a fun-lover to give lengthy attention to art, as Alice had hinted once to him, it made little difference at the time. For actually, it was this same fun-seeking attitude that brought James to one of those critical passes in life that was to force him into art.

It was one of those summer days, hot and severe on three cow-boys who had whooped-it-up at a Reno club the night before. James, Elmer and Fred were loafing on the back porch of the Conradt house, tossing ideas about what they should do. Fred perked up with the thought of using his three broncs to put on local bucking horse shows and then take up a collection.

Alice thought the idea was silly when they explained it at the supper table that night. But the 111's were restless and wanted something to do other than roaming around the Reno clubs. Alice's father suggested they get themselves jobs, a suggestion which was completely passed over by them.

To paraphrase an expression, James had two important horses in his life: Smoky, the blue roan that would inspire him to write the classic book of that name, and Happy, a black bronc that finally finished James as a bronc rider and brought him closer to Alice and art.

Fred's other two horses were named Hell-Morgan and Soleray.

The 111 bantered about as to who was to get which horse. James shied away from Hell-Morgan. That horse had been used in the Reno rodeo a few months before, had done a fair job of tossing his riders, and James had hinted to his partners that he was avoiding any more rough horses. So he selected Happy, while Fred drew Hell-Morgan and Elmer, Soleray.

James and Elmer decided to ride their horses and get the feel of them before trailing them to likely areas where they could gather an audience. With them went Fred's brother, Gus, to take some pictures to be used on a publicity poster.

Fred ran the horses into the corral. James roped Happy and started to throw his saddle on the horse. When James described this saddle, years later, he admitted that he had known better than to use that saddle. Having decided to stay off rough horses, he had purchased a roping type after his discharge from the army, which was hardly adequate for bronc riding.

"The boys," said James, "used to kid me about the cantle, saying all it was good for was to keep a feller from setting down."[5]

Actually it wasn't the cantle that caused some thoughts in James' mind — it was the pair of twenty-six inch tapaderos that hung from the stirrups. A menacing hunch had come to him that he should remove them before saddling Happy. But the hunch wasn't strong enough, and James told Fred to ear Happy down while he threw the saddle on. Besides, Fred had said that Happy was only an average bucking horse, and considered him easy pickings for James. What Fred and James failed to consider was that Happy hadn't been ridden for nearly three months. and had had a lot of time to "stack up on orneriness."

While Fred eared Happy down, James slipped into the saddle

[5]James relates, reliably, about Happy in *All in the Day's Riding*.

and settled himself firmly. He indicated to Fred to let go of the
hold on Happy's ears. Immediately the horse leaped into a series
of hard pile-driving jolts. James followed the rhythm of Happy's
tactics, and figured that Happy would be a breeze to ride. Maybe
Happy sensed James' overconfident attitude for, at that moment,
the horse came to a shuffling stop, and bowed his neck. Instead of
making a hard, forward jump as James expected, Happy went up
and whirled in a backward spin, throwing James' rhythm and
timing into a clash. Happy whirled again, and James lost his left
stirrup. He reached for the saddlehorn, while his foot fished for
the stirrup which the tapadero was swinging like a kite.

James admits he was putting on a bum ride, but he stuck to
Happy as best he could. The horse floated from hard jolts to
easy crow hops and it felt to James that Happy was about ready
to run. Heavy timber lay ahead and James decided this was as
good a time as any to hop off just in case Happy planned to
clear the timber out of his way. James braced himself on the
saddle, and prepared to swing his right leg over the saddle. Just
as he began to ease off, James spied the railroad tracks, flashing
glares of light from the sun. He changed his mind and started to
settle back in the saddle until after Happy had detoured away
from the tracks. It happened quickly. While James was half in
and half out of the saddle, Happy maneuvered from his crow-
hopping and leaped into another series of pile-driving jolts. The
last jolt chucked James, and he landed between the railroad
tracks with his head hitting one of the rails. That was all he
remembered.

A doctor was called, and for the thirty minutes James was
unconscious, his torn scalp was temporarily bandaged. The doctor
told Fred that further treatment was needed at the hospital. As
James' unconsciousness waned, Fred and Elmer helped him to
stand upright. While they steadied him, James began to sing,
Oh Bury Me Not On the Lone Prairie. There was a broad grin

on his face, and one of the spectators who had gathered, commented: "He's out of his head."

James looked to the man, and answered, "You'd be out of your head too, if you tried to bend a railroad track with it."

Chapter Four

TWENTY-TWO stitches in his scalp, and a concussion, forced James to a bed rest of about two weeks. After two days in the hospital he was released, since Fred had offered his room to James for the remainder of his convalescence.

The accident and its near fatal consequences shook James to rock bottom, and started him thinking about himself. He was now twenty-seven years old, with nothing to show but a lot of drifting and tomfoolery. Alice was no less severe on James than she was on her brother Fred about his lack of responsibility.

While James did stay in bed and sketched for hours, his thoughts were heavy in self-reflection. In the past he had been bone-broken and busted as a bronc string rider, and as a continued future, he realized the broncs would get the best of him. He was acquainted with enough old timers who were once agile and top buckeroos like himself. While some were lucky, and found a pet position on some ranch where they could spend the rest of their lives, far too many were lost souls, drinking heavily and just existing instead of living.

Alice spent considerable time in conversation with James while he rested in the Conradt house. She didn't particularly care for James when she first met him, although since his accident, he seemed a lot gentler and more pleasant than he had at first appeared. They talked about horses, and especially his hopes to study art. Alice was in accord with his wish, and this opened the way for James to talk more about himself.

James talked freely with Alice. She was a good listener, and she caught her first glimmer of the romantic sentiment James had for the west. He bemoaned the way the country had changed; railroads, fences, sheep and foreigners to herd them, and engine-power that was sweeping the horse off the farms and ranches. After a while he even talked in detail about himself being an orphan, losing Bopy, and being a drifting cowboy all of his life.

One of James' frequent and favored talks with Alice was what she called his *log cabin talk*. It even crops up in James' writings ever so often, with only the slightest provocation of a lead. When he would get moody, he would talk about having a cabin some-where in the pines, with a brook running by, a few head of horses about the place, and a studio where he could draw and even try painting.

In the weeks during James' convalescence, Alice found herself becoming as anxious for his aspirations as James seemed to be. She wanted to care for him and to be part of the man for whom she was feeling an ever-closer association. When at last he talked specifically about going to an art school in San Francisco, Alice agreed, and told him "by all means stop riding bucking horses."

Alice's mother had also become fond of James, and encouraged Alice to marry him. Alice's father, however, was still cool to James. Without voicing his opinion, his attitude reflected that he didn't care for the attentions James and Alice were exchanging. He did tell his wife that Alice was too young to even think about a serious courtship with a man over ten years her senior. And besides, James hadn't really shown himself to be anything more than a loafing cowboy.

James and Alice realized that art school was the best move he could now make. Not only for himself, but to show Alice's father that he, James, did have better motives in life.

In August of 1919, James arranged to go to San Francisco and enroll in the California School of Fine Arts. He planned also to see the editors of *Sunset Magazine* in San Francisco, which at the time was a natural media for James' subject art. James hocked his saddle for train fare and, before boarding the train, Fred and Elmer handed James the few dollars they had. James refused, but Fred insisted. "Hell, take it. You know where we'll spend it anyhow."

In September, James registered for evening classes in art school, and took a small apartment on Howard Street. About the same time he found a convenient job as usher in a movie theater, where he worked the matinee shift. His routine settled into morning art practice, his job in the afternoon, and school in the evening. Shortly thereafter, and either through the school or by his own connections, James did some advertising posters for the Bear Furniture Company and one for the Levi-Strauss Company, makers of denim pants. The latter poster showed two bear cubs each on a leg of the pants trying to pull them apart.

While these assignments were encouraging to James, school was becoming an ordeal. The discipline of still-life studies, and the repetition of practice, became too stilted and somber for his crisp, free style. His interest waned, and one evening the instructor noticed his lack of interest in the nude model. He asked James why he was not sketching. James answered, "If I'm to draw udders, I'd rather draw them on cows than on nice ladies."[1]

Another evening, and as a guest of the instructor, Lee Rice visited to view and comment on the students' work. Rice, a noted artist and writer for horse magazines, was previously a bluebrush vaquero from California. Looking over the class, his eyes halted on the bowlegged fellow wearing cowboy boots. Rice walked to James' desk and peered over his shoulder. The class was sketching a human figure, and James' efforts were something

[1]Bob Cormack, "Will James," *Denver Westerners Brand Book*, 1962.

of an insult to the female model, as Rice recalls. But along the margins of James' sketchbook were small drawings of cowboys riding bucking horses. Rice was also wearing the symbol of his breed, boots, and immediately James and Rice struck a natural accord as fellow travelers of the range country.

They became friendly, and saw each other frequently. After class James and Rice would usually meet in some small restaurant and talk art, Charlie Russell, Remington, and tell tales of their experiences as cowboys.

Rice was acquainted with Maynard Dixon, a good artist, and popular illustrator. He introduced James to Dixon.

Unlike James' meeting with Russell, Dixon was outgoing, friendly and encouraging with advice that may have been another turning point in James' life. Dixon studied the cow country sketches James had brought with him. He also studied James' technique by asking him to sketch a bucking horse for him. Afterwards, Dixon advised James to quit art school. The instructional methods of the school, with its emphasis on preliminary sketching, might ruin rather than help what Dixon considered James' natural gift. Dixon noticed too that James did nothing that was either academic or conventional in his techniques. Instead, he drew directly without preliminary sketching, and with immediate results in his mind. Thus James was able to put a complete and thorough idea on paper in a matter of minutes.

Art school could probably have helped James in drawing human figures (his are notoriously absent of necks) but the risk was that it might have ruined his own free style. James dropped out of art school shortly thereafter.

Dixon and James became steady companions, along with Rice, and rode horseback together in the nearby hills. Dixon's advice and criticism were good medication for James' confidence, to the extent that James felt eager to approach the *Sunset* editorial office.

James probably would have been turned down in his request to see Joseph Henry Jackson, then an assistant editor, if he had not presented a letter of introduction from a mining friend of Jackson's whom James met in the hospital after Happy had dumped him. The miner and western buff, who had a bed next to James, was impressed with James' sketchings, and he may have been the person who first slipped the thought to James about going to art school. In any case, it did get James into Jackson's office. But Jackson wasn't too impressed with James' portfolio.

"We couldn't use such drawings as these," James reports Jackson as saying. "They would have to be a lot better. Come around again some other time."

"When?" James asked.

"Oh, in a few months or so, when you have something else to show me."

James learned later that Jackson liked his style and had felt that if James were really interested in art and in illustrating for the magazine, he would come back, showing improvement through greater effort.

Having been shunned by Jackson and with it any hopes for selling his sketches, James turned his thoughts momentarily to another job, since he had quit the movie house some time back. The only job listing requiring no experience was a riveter's helper on the dry docks in the shipyards. In his letters to Alice, James complained how discouraging it was to work so close to people, that his eyes could hardly stretch themselves for a healthy look to an horizon. "I don't like steel and soot," he wrote. "I like flesh and dust. . ."

Before the letter even arrived in Reno, James had quit the job. He'd been feeling groggy and dizzy, and at first he thought the dizziness was caused by the height of the scaffolds. But then pain whirled in his head. James feared he might fall, and so he quit the day after he had started.

That evening in his room, the pains became severe. He tossed for a while and then slept. When he awoke he felt something wrong with his eyes. A burning sensation was causing them to water profusely. He turned on the light switch, but was jolted by a sense of darkness. Presumably, the injury when Happy tossed James onto the railroad track, became agitated through the riveting vibrations and caused temporary semi-blindness. For some hours he stayed alone in his room, completely unnerved by his blurred sight. Later, as the pain subsided, his sight returned.

Once over the shock, James completed a series of cow country sketches for *Sunset Magazine*. He returned to Jackson's office about a month after his first visit. Jackson thumbed through the sketches, which depicted tragedy and comedy vignettes of animals on the range. He bought two for twenty-five dollars each. Others Jackson promised to buy once James made a few changes.

One Man Horse, which James says was a portrait of himself and his horse Smoky, appeared full page in the January 1920 issue of *Sunset*. From then on, with the exception of about a year, James' work would appear in print the rest of his life.

Chapter Five

INITIAL success had come relatively easy to James. If not a tribute to the proverbial persistence which characterizes many artists and writers before receiving wide acceptance, then definitely it is a tribute to James' natural talent which was developing a sparkling quality all its own.

Jackson took personal pride as the first editor to recognize James' art, and when James was nationally known a few years later, Jackson wrote in his *Across the Editor's Desk:*[1]

"... To find, develop and bring out new talent is the favorite sport of every editorial office. Rare talent is so scarce that its discovery causes as much joy around the desk as the arrival of Santa Claus in a house full of children. Therefore, Will James with his half-dozen crude but vivid drawings was received with open arms...

"This lean youngster with the tang of the sagebrush still clinging to him made good because he carried into his drawings — and into his writing — the unadulterated flavor of the desert and mountain, because the subtle essence of that spiritual attitude which we call the Far West pervaded everything he did.

"We are proud of Will James and we are patting ourselves on the back ... for having roped, tied and broken him for the role in the arena of arts and letters ..."

[1]*Sunset Magazine,* December, 1924.

Practically every month, James had a full page sketch in *Sunset*, usually with an editor's note as ... "The artist has had no training in art, but he has remarkable natural talent from years of life as a cowboy and a sympathetic knowledge of the actors in such a tragedy."

James sold a batch of drawings at a time with a simple title under each. His more popular drawings were: *Mothers*, an adult cow and bear with young meeting with startled expression on a mountain trail; *Friend in Disguise*, a sketch of a lion ready to attack a horse, but who is saved by a snake rattling in the brush, and the popular *Keno, the Cowhorse*, a series of nine sketches depicting the life of a cow pony.

All his pictures told a simple story about the ways of animals, and are generous evidence of an observing eye in James. Along with his own sketches, Jackson assigned James to illustrate a series of range poems by E. C. Lincoln, and these appeared periodically. But when James had to slant his sketches to the thought of another writer they never seem to have the feel in them that he had in his own.

Flushed with the acceptance of his work and a steady income for a refreshing change, James plunged wholeheartedly into art. He moved to Sausalito to be with the local art colony and seemingly, he tried to change his *breed* and brush shoulders with those aspirants to the art world. But they revolted him because of what he felt was an artificial atmosphere which they created for themselves. From then on, James shied away from academic art and artists, and none of the old masters would mean anything to him. Only the works of Russell, and to a lesser degree, Remington, were masters to him, and James studied them diligently. In April 1920, James wrote Russell, and sent a sketch along with his letter, asking advice and criticism. Russell replied:[2]

[2]*Good Medicine—The Illustrated Letters of Charles M. Russell.*

May 12, 1920

Hello Will James

I got your letter and sketch and from it and other worke
I have seen of yours in Sunset I know you have felt a horse
under you. Nobody can tell you how to draw a horse ore cow.

I never got to be a bronk rider but in my youthfull days
wanted to be and while that want lasted I had a fine chance
to study hoss enatimy from under and over . . . the under
was the view a taripan gits. The over while I hovered ont
the end of a Macarty rope was like the eagle sees grand but
dam scary for folks without wings.

James, you say you havnt used color much dont be afraid
of paint I think its easier than eather pen ore pensol

I was down in Cal this winter and saw some fine ground
for cow pictures rolling country green with patches of
poppies and live oak mountain ranges with white peaks that
streach away to no where   I have never seen this kind of
country used in cow pictures   Why dont you try it . . .

James as I said before use paint but dont get smeary let
sombody elce do that keep on making real men horses and
cows of corse the real artisitick may never know you but
nature loving regular men will and thair is more of the last
kind in this old world an thair the kind you want to shake
hands with . . .

With best wishes to yourself and any who know me

Yours

C. M. RUSSELL

In June of 1920, Alice and her mother went to Sausalito to
visit Alice's sister, Annie, who was living there with a girl friend.
In her letters to Alice she wrote that James was somewhat lonely,
and spent most of his time in his cottage.

James was overjoyed when Alice arrived. For the first few
hours he did nothing but talk of art, Jackson, and future plans.
He had told her most of them in his letter, but she listened to
them again. For the first time he spoke of marriage, and also about
wanting to go back to Nevada. He didn't like the city. "Concrete
don't set with my soles like the desert does," he told her.

James did come back the following month after the visit of Alice and her mother. One month later, on July 7, 1920, Alice and James were married in Reno. She was sixteen and he, twenty-eight.

A honeymoon was waived for the time being since money was scarce. They returned to Sausalito where James finished some drawings for *Sunset*. Soon after, *Sunset* had a substantial back-log of drawings from James, and told him that would be all they could use for some time. Although an illustrating assignment came from the magazine office now and then, it was more than apparent that he and Alice soon would run out of money unless he could persuade other magazines to use his work.

James studied the east coast magazines more closely. As always, he was annoyed at the obvious lack of first-hand knowledge on the part of their western story illustrators. He felt certain that if once he could gain the favor of one magazine, others would turn to him. He told Alice that success with the eastern publishers could mean a place of their own; off by themselves, with horses, some cattle, and a studio for his work. That dream, however, needed tangible substance, and James hoped to achieve it by having his work accepted by eastern magazines.

He assembled a portfolio of sketches and cover ideas for a western pulp publishing chain, and sent them to New York. They were all promptly returned. He tried two other eastern magazines, and again his portfolio was sent back. His mood began to change and reflect a pensive meditation that confused Alice in helping him. He didn't want any help, but only to be left alone. Discouraged, James wanted to go back to Nevada and cowboy work. It was a rationalization, a return to something in which he felt more secure. Alice offered little advice or opinion in countering James' motives and contemplated moves. In the first few years of their marriage, she believed all he had told her, and abided by whatever he decided as being best for both of them.

Still, she was astute enough to recognize some weaknesses in his temperament, but had also as quickly learned not to confront James with them. Once she had suggested, in Sausalito, that he write about Bopy. James flatly replied that the idea was asinine. He was an artist, he said, and not a writer.

In the meantime, James had written to a rancher in Arizona that Elmer Freel said might be looking for some help at one of his line camps. James specified to the rancher that broncs were out of his working line. To James' surprise, the rancher replied that all he needed was someone to live at a line camp, where horses and cattle on the range came for water.

Mostly, it was a stock-watching job — checking the water, setting out salt, and doctoring any stock that needed attention. The job seemed ideal to James and Alice, and one where he obviously could still devote time to his art. James wrote a letter of acceptance.

From Sausalito they went to Reno for a brief visit with Alice's family, and then took the train to Arizona. Near the middle of the night James and Alice, according to the rancher's instructions, had the brakeman stop the train at the water tank outside of Kingman. At a small ranch near the water tank, James was to announce himself.

A light glowed invitingly from the distance, and James and Alice took off in its direction. They were made welcome and invited to stay the night. Early the next morning their host drove Alice and James to the line camp, completely stocked with food, and a letter of instructions.

This was a new experience for Alice. Although she had grown up in a desert state, she had always lived within city limits. Now, fifteen miles from anywhere, and with all sorts of shy creatures crawling along the ground and startling her, she was frightened. James was completely at ease, however, as though it had always been his home. He told her about the snakes, the Gila monsters, and some of the spiders and scorpions that inhabit the Arizona country. She cried one time, and accused him of trying to frighten her. But he informed her that the only way she could protect herself was to understand the nature of the creatures and, if he should be away, how to care for herself if bitten.

He also attempted to teach her how to shoot a pistol. After a while, he suggested to her that she had best try and hide rather than "shoot it out."

Their billet was a large one-room cabin with a stove and bed, bench chairs, and outside toilet. One corner of the cabin held their cache of flour, sugar, dried fruit and canned goods. Cooking was no problem to Alice, as she had learned early in her life how to assemble meals with minimum selection of foods.

Twice a day, cattle and horses would wander into the camp for water from the spring, and James inspected them at every visit. Other times, after the necessary chores of getting firewood or butchering a calf (James jerked most of the meat), he worked at his easel outside the cabin. Often James showed Alice the Russell reproductions he always carried with him and would explain to her what he was trying to do, and with a typical nod of his head when he was impressed with something, he showed her the excellence he found in Russell's work.

Although mail was infrequent, James did get a few more illustrating assignments from *Sunset*. Enos Mills, naturalist and writer, had submitted articles to the magazine which *Sunset* wanted James to illustrate. The articles and the drawings were later published in book form.

Alice never did feel completely happy at the line camp. She had adapted herself to the isolation, and even sensed some of the beauty which James himself saw in the lonely quiet. But she still felt lonely. James seemed to be aloof to her, except when he wanted to talk. Otherwise, he was at his art or in deep, silent thought. To the ways that a woman likes attention and compliments, James was oblivious. Alice cried numerous times when alone in the cabin, or when she took walks out into the desert by herself.

In the evenings, however, he was more sociable. He talked his *log cabin* talk, a place for him and Alice, or he would reminisce about his past life. Alice encouraged him to talk, as it seemed to draw him out of his melancholy, and awakened in her a sense that he did need her.

After three months, the stock of food dwindled, and James began to wonder if his employer had forgotten them. A few days later, the stores were practically exhausted.

"Well, the hell with him," declared James. The next morning they packed their bags, and walked to the neighbor that had driven them to the line camp.

Chapter Six

IN KINGMAN, James collected his back pay at the ranch's headquarters office. Without any ideas as to what he and Alice were
to do next, he took her to a small Mexican restaurant where they
sat and talked about their next move. Alice was apprehensive
about their meager savings, and proposed that they return to
Reno and stay with her parents. Mother would be happy to have
them, she added, and James could find a part time job and still
have time for his art.

James listened, but had no intentions of returning to Reno.
And as to Alice's offer that they stay at the home of her parents,
particularly since her father only mildly approved of James'
marriage to Alice, "that isn't in this boy's deck of cards as long as
I'm dealing," he told her.

James wanted to go to Santa Fe, where there was an art colony,
and since the area was good ranching country, he felt assured of
a job. After explaining his desire, he said to her, "Saddle up for
Santa Fe!"

Alice thought he meant to buy two horses and ride all the way
to New Mexico, and she began to express doubt of his proposal.
"That would take days and days," she said.

"Your think tank must be emptying out," James joked. "New
Mexico is only a couple of days east."

Alice stared with a hint of annoyance at James. "*I* went to school, Bill," she said sharply. "I know were New Mexico is and to go there by horseback will take *days and days!*"

James rolled back in his chair and laughed. "Poor, little city girl," he teased, "just knows only that book English."

He explained to Alice that his remark to *saddle up* meant to travel — and not necessarily by horseback.

They boarded the train that afternoon for Santa Fe.

An intrinsic light and landscape had attracted artists to a small colony in Santa Fe. Even today it is a haven for artists. To James, Santa Fe was the west for which he had always felt a stirring affection; where the sky belonged only to God, and no man-made symbols of his abilities poked through it.

"Whenever I get around country like this," he said to Alice, "I feel as little as an ant. The bigger the country, the littler I feel, and the happier I am."

Alice was learning with sharp perception that the land determines the nature of some men, and for James, the open country — the desert, the mountains — exhilarated his blood and cleared his mind of self doubts and inhibitions. He was eager and intense to paint. These were good omens, for the dreams and hopes he had for himself and Alice and the complexities that were due for his life had not yet blocked and frustrated his dreams. Unlike Sausalito, Santa Fe's cultural and social atmosphere was horses and cowboys, ranches and pleasing country. Life there was indolently comfortable for mind and body.

A turn of luck greeted Alice and James when they came to Santa Fe in 1921. A studio apartment in the former governor's mansion had been vacated by an artist, only hours before their arrival. It offered a beautiful, deep view to the west, far across the desert and into the hills. Sunset became a time for James and Alice to sit outside and watch the painted evening skies. Alice remembers that at no other time did James express so much inspiration, ambition and utter peace with himself. Not even their dwindling cash could upset him. For Alice, too, the months there were idyllic. James was in a rare mood, sharing his thoughts with her, affectionate and attentive.

While other artists painted landscapes or the Mexican element of Santa Fe, James was unique with his cowboys and their horses and his general renditions of the cow country. Unique not only by singular emphasis, but too, in a technique and style that was impressive. James made some minor sales to visiting tourists and local ranchers who wanted a series of sketches or a painting. One day, an unassuming gentleman offered James $200 for a painting. Later, James found out, the gentleman was the governor. It had happened quickly, spurring Alice and James to celebrate that evening. The sale excited James to a pitch of restlessness, as Alice recalls, but he was wise enough apparently, to comment that there are bound to be "a lot of ups and downs."

It wasn't much later in the year when the down trend brought them to another serious conference on their immediate future. Their finances were little, and the few sales James had made with his art weren't adequate to sustain them.

Seemingly, fate was again weaving a close pattern in James' life. If Maynard Dixon's counsel for James to quit art school was the first important acquaintance and advice, then the entry of the Springer brothers into James' life is the second and most influencing.

The Springer family were pioneers in the northern New Mexico Territory, and the family line still persists in that part of the country around Cimarron and Springer. Frank Springer, lawyer and paleontologist, was one of the principal contributors in supporting the art museum in Santa Fe. Two sons, Wallace and Edward, followed art and ranching respectively. It was Wallace who in his constant ramblings in the art colony became attracted to the ranch and horse scenes James displayed. Because of similar interests in ranching and art, a friendship grew immediately, and Wallace frequently visited James and Alice for long evening talks.

When James realized that he would have to obtain work, he approached Wallace and asked if there was a possibility for a job on his brother's ranch. Wallace replied that he was going to the ranch shortly, and for James to come along. Something, Wallace assured James, would be found for him to do.

They went to the CS Ranch in Cimarron a few days later. Wallace explained privately to his brother Ed, "This boy knows his riggin', but he's on his uppers, and I want to help him out." Wallace told also about James having been hurt by a horse sometime back and to give James something easy to do. Ed replied that he would.

Ed Springer had already sent the bulk of his riders up to a mountain camp 9500 feet high in the Cimarron range. Ed decided to make James a general caretaker around the camp, with the understanding that James could still work at his art. The latter was a point Wallace had suggested because James had considerable talent, and he didn't want him to neglect that work.

James held his head low when Ed outlined the proposal. Ed studied James' expressions and detected that what he had said wasn't sitting comfortably with James. Finally, after some prompting by Ed, James admitted he wanted to ride with the boys — no broncs — but to help with the cow work. Ed acceded to James' wish, more for Wallace's favor than because of any particular faith in James' ability as a cowhand, of which Ed knew nothing.

With the job determined, James requested a few days to take care of his affairs in Santa Fe. Ed told him to report back when he was ready.

Late that same evening when James returned to Santa Fe, he told Alice of the job and that it would be best if she returned to Reno for a while. Alice did not want to go, but James insisted that he could not take her to a cow camp. She asked to stay in Santa Fe, and James countered that the added expenses would keep them broke. She said she would get a job, and James cut that thought without any refining of his language. Finally Alice consented to the logic of James' wish, and at the railroad depot the next day they separated for the first time.

When James reported back to the CS Ranch, acting straw boss John Brewer cut James a gentle string of horses and they rode to the mountain camp. It wasn't long afterwards that James proved his worth as a cowhand. He wasn't sorting wits with broncs, but on round-up he was roping, branding and vaccinating. As Ed Springer remembers, James mixed easily with the cowhand breed. Topping that, James drew pictures for them, pen and ink sketches mostly, that soon were numerous enough to appear as sheets of wallpaper on the bunkhouse walls. James drew his sketches effortlessly, says Springer, and one could summarize that James knew the twists of a bucking horse.

About the middle of summer, around July, Ed rode into camp with two companions; Jack Narin, who had a house nearby on the Urracca Ranch, and Burton Twichell, Dean of Students at Yale University. The trio were on their annual hunting trip in the mountains.

In the days that followed, James made a considerable impression on Ed and his friends. They had first wondered who the artist was, and during the evenings they sat with absorbed interest as James became a storyteller, with a parcel of range and horse stories. He told his stories much as he was to write them, in the cowboy jargon, convincingly and interestingly. And if a story lent itself to illustrating, James would sketch the particular twisting actions of a bronc as he talked. He never spoke about his past except as it related to a job at a ranch "up north" or to chasing mustangs in Nevada. To Ed and Jack, James was a cowboy different from the common mixture. To Burton Twichell, who was conditioned to evaluating talents and potentialities of students at Yale, James had more to offer than being a cowboy the rest of his life. A few times, Burton singled out James for short talks with him, and questioned James as to what he intended to do with his talent. James said he wanted to be an artist and to paint the west as it really was.

One evening, in Ed's tent, Burton and Jack were commenting about James when Burton said, "Ed, I have a scholarship at the university that just fits Bill. It's for artists who aren't qualified to enter by the usual scholarship requirements. You think Bill would be interested?"

Ed summoned James the next morning and told him what Burton had suggested. James was interested, even excited about the prospects. Later, when details of the scholarship were outlined by Burton, James began to demur. The scholarship covered only the university fees and James admitted he had no savings to carry him through. He thanked the three men for their interest and left the tent.

The next day while the trio were riding to Jack's home, Ed told Burton to reserve that scholarship for Bill and that he (Ed) and Jack would stake Bill for any expenses while learning.

When James rode down from the camp to the ranch on a mail run, Ed called him aside, and told him that Burton would reserve the scholarship, and that he and Jack would stake James' expenses. "We feel," said Ed, "that you're a good investment — and if you pan out, you can pay us back."

James accepted the offer eagerly, and wired Alice he was coming to Reno with some good news.

FAMILY PORTRAIT

a time of innocence, but in the seed of time of stress, Will James at the knee of
father, Jean Dufault. James was nine years old and already displaying art
nts that would lead him to the West. Auguste is next to his mother. Standing
are his sisters Eugènie, left, and Helene.

— *Courtesy of Auguste Dufault.*

49

MAN OF THE WEST

In his first year in western Canada, James was all buckeroo, but
only in appearance. Taken at a cow camp on Sage Creek (in
Alberta close to the northeastern Montana border) in 1907.

— *Courtesy of Eleanor Snook.*

THE LAST DAYS OF AN OLD ACT

A range boss instructing his riders at round-up time. Taken about 1917 in eastern Nevada, James (left) caught the tail-end of horse culture on the range and the ranch.

— *Courtesy of Eleanor Snook.*

51

When Two Careers Meet

James' finish as a rider, and his beginning as a serious artist. *Happy,* the horse, changed the course of James' life. Taken about a half-hour after James landed head-first on a railroad track from the back of *Happy.*

— Courtesy of Dolly Conradt.

52

THE III's (ONE-ELEVENS)
Elmer, James and Fred, in Reno, 1919.
— *Courtesy of Dolly Conradt.*

53

RIDING ROUGH AND READY

James is on the dark horse, from this still of an early western movie. About 19

— *Courtesy of Eleanor Snook.*

WILD AND WOOLLY
Working a horse at the Fat Jones stable in Hollywood. James'
first excursion to Hollywood was in 1916.

— *Courtesy of Eleanor Snook.*

55

AT THE WASHOE VALLEY CABIN

In the Washoe Valley, north of Carson City, Alice and James had the cabin that they had so often talked about. Here, James wrote *Smoky*, one of his most famous and popular books.

— *Courtesy of Dolly Conradt.*

ALICE

— *Courtesy of Dolly Conradt.*

57

THE CABIN IN WASHOE VALLEY

— *Courtesy of Dolly Conradt.*

"THE PRODIGAL'S RETURN"

One of the many full page sketches that James sold to *Sunset Magazine*. Each was a vignette, complete in itself.

— *Courtesy Sunset Magazine.*

MORE COWBOY THAN ARTIST

At time of this drawing, he was neither cowboy nor artist. James
sketched it while making use of time in Nevada State Prison.

— *Courtesy Nevada State Prison.*

THE NEVADA ROUND-UP

RENO'S ANNUAL CARNIVAL OF THE RANGE

Featuring Exhibition Performers, and Contests for All Comers in the Daring and Skillful Feats of the Cattle Country

$5000 IN PRIZES

Include Reno in Your Over-the-Fourth Vacation and Enjoy the Biggest Fourth of July Show in the West

For Bucking, Roping, Riding, Racing and Bull-Riding Contests

COMING!

RENO, NEV., JULY 1-2-3-4-5, '20

"Let 'er Buck" and "Let's Go" (Write Reno Chamber of Commerce or Mayor H. E. Stewart for Particulars)

EARLY ART

In 1919, James sold his first art. He received fifty dollars for this drawing, which was used on posters and magazine advertising.

WILL JAMES ON ONE OF HIS HORSES AT HIS WASHOE VALLEY ACREAGE IN NEV
The ranch is now a camp for young people during the summer, where Ja
books are available, and film version of *Smoky* is shown during encampm
— *Courtesy of Eleanor Snook.*

Book Party

h his inevitable cigarette and two books to his credit, James, as shown in this
ure, frequently gave talks and signed books in Reno and San Francisco.

— *Courtesy of Eleanor Snook.*

THE ROCKING R

Rocking R in Montana became the embodiment of James' incarnation of the old

Chapter Seven

AT FIRST THOUGHT, it appears difficult to justify James' wish
to study art again. Still fresh in his mind was the letdown of art
school in California, and the advice of Maynard Dixon which
James never took lightly. Very likely, in private conversation
with Burton, he told James that it would be an opportunity for
him to meet some of the editors with whom Burton was acquainted in New York. Since this is what did happen, the reason
for James going to Yale Art School seems logical.

James went to Reno to see Alice before going to Connecticut.
She was delighted to see him so shortly after she had accepted the
probable fact that they would be separated for some time. But
she gave the idea of his going to Yale a cool reception. It meant
separation again, and she wondered how Yale could be any more
helpful for James than was the school in San Francisco. James
told her that he felt this was a good move for him, and if the
skies looked a little brighter back that way, he would send for
her as soon as he could. He stayed with Alice's parents for two
days, and the reunion with Fred and Elmer and their respective
girl friends, Dolly and Betty (a lady bronc rider), and the Conradt family was a stimulating welcome to James. He told them
at supper one evening that, never having a family of his own,
it gave him a mighty fine feeling to be part of this one. Even
Alice's father was warming to James.

At New Haven, Connecticut, James enrolled in art and English A, a prerequisite course for any entering student. The old traditions settled by time at Yale were an interesting side of life James had never seen before. His first few letters to Alice were filled with a rapid pace about new sights and expectations. A week after his arrival, however, the Yale tradition seemed to press in on him and immediately his letters to Alice indicated dark clouds rather than the hopeful bright days he had anticipated. His emotions, he felt, were shackled and he was lonely, depressed, and art school was art school, west coast or east coast. But most of all, besides Alice, he missed the desert, the hills and the stock grazing.

This was one of the intense emotions of Will James, and it is a vital probing tool in understanding what has been called the James enigma. The land made him a loner, and when depressed he invariably would want to ride into the desert. Whatever it was that stirred him, he felt humble and content where nature abounded. In the coming years when the Jameses and the Conradts moved to James' Montana ranch, Alice and Dolly sensed his emotional drama, and often watched him walking alone in the foothills that surrounded his ranch. Other times, he would sit on a rock or the corral fence and roll cigarette after cigarette and lose his thoughts and whatever was pressing him, by letting his eyes rest on the trees and mountains and stock grazing peacefully nearby. In the early 1940's, when James was visiting a friend, Dick Dickson, in Palm Springs, Dickson showed James a book long forgotten and written by a cowboy named Bob Beverly. Dickson recalls that James pointed out a particular paragraph to him and commented, "This cowboy knows the same feeling that gets me." The paragraph read:

> "The cowboy of the old west worked in a land that seemed to be grieving over something — a kind of sadness, loneliness in a deathly quiet. One not acquainted with the plains

could not understand what effect it had on the mind. It produced a heartache and a sense of exile."[1]

As a romanticist and a sentimentalist, James was filled with nostalgia at the thought of the Golden Age of the cow country. Although he knew only a small part of that era, it intensified an emotion and an attitude that Alice never could comprehend. It did produce a sense of exile for James, a moodiness that took him off by himself. For Alice, a sense of inadequacy came upon her when James acted as he did. But this was only one of his enigmas that perplexed her. There would be others, and all would be a rival against which Alice could never seem to compete.

At the moment, however, his letters from Connecticut were outpourings of loneliness and of disappointment with art school.

Yet James had his good moments while in Connecticut. Burton took paternal interest in James' progress, and invited James to eat at his home many times. At the university James roomed with another artist named Webb Overlander[2] who didn't particularly care for James because "James threw the bull too much." Nonetheless, they did spend some time together, and Overlander recalls his acquaintance by a few incidents.

"I remember one time we were in a cellar on campus doing some week-end work for the school when James came upon some Remington prints that were stacked away. He sat there for hours studying them and smoking his Bull Durham cigarettes one after another. I finally finished my work and waited for him. But after a while got tired of waiting, and left him there. I don't think he even heard me say I was going."

James also began to drink again when he was at Yale. He often did when he was lonely. As a cowboy, he did his fair share of drying-up bottles, but since marrying Alice he rarely drank liquor.

[1]*Hobo of the Rangeland,* Bob Beverly, c 1940, New Mexico.
[2]Personal make-up man for movie star, John Wayne.

Overlander recalls that James put on a couple of *dillies*.

"One time, he came into the dorm drunk as hell. He was sort of half-crying while muttering something under his breath. All I could make out was something about a murder in Canada; Alberta I believe he said. But he had fooled them and burned the log cabin jail and escaped."

Overlander thought it was just another of James' tall tales and never gave it a second thought. James would slip with that remark again to Alice at their Montana ranch while he was drunk. Significance of the story will be discussed further on.

His letters to Alice were daily arrivals. After two weeks of school, he wrote her that he was quitting. Completely upset by his actions and knowing he was lonely, Alice borrowed money from her father and went to New Haven. In the meantime, James explained to Burton that he could no longer tolerate art school. He wanted to do what he felt he had to do, and art school was artificial, frustrating and a hobble to himself. Moreover, he wanted a studio of his own where he could work. James was completely confident that he could produce good and salable material as he had done for *Sunset Magazine*. But he needed better markets.

Burton was sympathetic to James' thoughts about art school. He sensed in James an anxiety and an impatience with anything that would shackle him from expressing what he wanted to portray on paper and canvas. James frequently showed Burton the historical errors of other illustrators in the New York magazines, and enjoyed discussing art with Burton, who a fancier and critic himself, challenged the interpretations of James' sketches and ideas. To a letter of 1922, in which Burton had criticized some sketches of James' cowboys, James answered:

"The criticism you handed me was good and I appreciate it by the fact that you wish me to keep improving — but I can say (not to stick up for my work, but only for the trueness of what

I put out) that in my drawings, even the cowboys may look long waisted. What makes him look that way is the way he wears his clothes. His waist line is below the hips. That's where his breeches and chap belt rests and what makes him look longer that way. Other folks wear theirs way up above the hips, but they don't have the freedom of movement the cowboy's got to have ... As for aquiline faces, sharp hook noses and such, you're right there. What I've done is put all the cowboys I've seen and known along with myself in the same pot and all boiled down I got one character what covers over seventy-five percent of the range riders, far as that goes all of us makes the same mistake if you call it such. You can tell a Russell, Remington, Leigh, Wyeth or Dixon cowboy far as you can see 'em ... they all got one character same as I got mine — it's just how they see the cowboy — it's why some are truer than others ..."

Burton had faith in James' judgment and, although he may have had some doubts about some of James' work, he believed James had the talent to make the top grade. Besides, James had said in a letter to Burton, "to win big, one has to play big stakes." The big stakes were the New York magazines. Burton made arrangements to take James to New York to meet some of the top magazine editors.

Meanwhile, Alice's arrival in New Haven was a surprise to James, as she wanted it to be. Officially James was dropped from the university, but was presently a house guest of the Twichells. They also welcomed Alice.

A few days later, Burton and James went to New York. James took along a portfolio of his best drawings to show Charles Dana Gibson, editor of the old *Life Magazine* which at the time used mostly illustrations instead of photographs. Gibson did not hesitate to heap verbal praise upon a glowing James and told him that his drawings had life in them. James commented he would rather have them in *Life*. They talked mostly about James' background and his natural propensity to art. Gibson expressed awe that James did not work from models. James explained what he was attempting to do — true visual representations of life in the west — as opposed to the mythical presentations that were more popular with magazines in the eastern part of the country. Gibson was impressed with the young man, and later confided to Burton that he could well understand why art school was too narrow for what James was trying to accomplish. Gibson outlined some criticisms, and told James to assemble a set of his drawings, as he had for *Sunset,* and to call again.

After leaving Gibson's office, James was bent on letting out a *war whoop.* Burton snuffed the urge by telling him they were in the wrong place.

A week later, James and Alice moved to New York, with some financial help from Burton, and found an apartment on West 86th Street. Gibson revived James' energies and stimulated him to work zealously. In his first letter to Burton written from New York, James wrote:

> "Yes sir it all looks mighty good — and to think that if you had not made that little trip to the Cimarron country and been the kind of man you are — I might be setting traps for a living this winter or else hazing a herd on the winter range."

James worked diligently on a set of sketches for *Life Magazine* and visited with Gibson again to see if these ideas were developing satisfactorily. Gibson restated his enthusiasm and a few days later, James submitted his portfolio. Gibson told him to come back after the next weekly editorial board meeting .

James patiently waited out the week. To Alice, he kidded about how they would spend all "that money *Life* would pay." When James returned, all he received was Gibson's regrets. The editorial board, explained Gibson, liked the sketches and saw much merit in them. But it wasn't quite what *Life's* editorial board felt suitable for their magazine.

Gibson expressed his personal disappointment, especially since he had led James to expect acceptance of whatever he submitted. He encouraged James to go on and emphasized that one magazine was not the whole publishing world.

Life's rejection had sapped James of a big bulk of his hopes. But he had no intentions of wallowing in the let-down. What annoyed and confused James was that he offered authentic sketches and he could find no reason why eastern magazines contented themselves with half-truths in the illustrations they did accept. James wrote Burton and expressed that what he would have to do with *Life* was to: "just educate them to it . . . to sketch something to their liking at first and then afterwards to submit my own feelings in the sketches. That was how I had done it with *Sunset.*"

James even made a $200 bet with Burton that within a year he would sell to *Life*. James would lose that bet, but only because within a year or so another magazine would be taking all he could offer.

Presently, however, he and Alice were almost broke. James still made occasional sales to *Sunset,* but there seemed little hope that he would derive enough sales from the magazine to allow him to stay in New York for further probing of the eastern magazine market. Burton had offered James a loan, but he declined since he had already discussed with Burton a loan in order to build a studio in Nevada.

While James was ever grateful to Burton for all his help and advice, it appeared to him that his entire New York venture was a discouraging setback for what he had anticipated. Sending him even further into depression was the beginning realization that his oil painting techniques could not stretch to the greatness he admired so much in Russell. The harder James worked in oils, the more he realized Russell's genius, and despaired to Alice of his own talent ever matching Russell's. It wasn't easy for

James to admit to himself that pen and pencil techniques could not easily be duplicated in grander presentation in oils. He said to Alice that it looked as if he had reached his plateau in oils. And he knew that level wasn't good enough.

For a few weeks James sulked around the apartment. Alice hinted that they must do something, even go back to Nevada before they were entirely broke. Maynard Dixon had in the meantime written James of some work for him with a calendar company. Also, *Sunset* might have more illustrating assignments if he were closer to San Francisco.

Spring was coming too. In New York it is measured mostly by the cessation of wind and snow. James saw it differently in his mind, and would remark to Alice now and then about "patches of grass peeking through the snow," "guess the cottonwoods are dressing out about now and the creeks beginning to break through the ice . . ."

He needed only a slight hint from Alice, and they were on their way back to Nevada.

Chapter Eight

RELUCTANTLY, James followed Alice's advice and moved into her parents' house. They more than welcomed them; even Alice's father indicated, through a paternal sort of interest, that he no longer was irritated with James for marrying Alice. But James felt he was imposing and that coming to the Conradt's was a sure indication he and Alice were in low tide. "I feel like a licked dog coming here," he told her.

In the summer of 1922 James went alone to San Francisco as Maynard Dixon's guest. James stayed for two weeks, and obtained sketching assignments from *Sunset Magazine* and some commercial art work for local business firms.

Meanwhile, Alice and her brother Paul looked for a place where she and James could live. Alice realized James was totally unhappy living in the Conradt house. Everyone was crowded and James had neither the quiet nor the space he needed to work.

Paul's familiarity with local conditions and its people brought to him word of a studio-type apartment for rent on the Couglin's Ranch west of Reno. The ranch was set upon a hillside, with rolling acres of sagebrush spreading around the entire ranch. When Paul took Alice to see the place, she was sure James would find it attractive. When James returned from San Francisco, he was as delighted as she had expected. Now, at least, he had a studio. They moved into their apartment and, shortly after, the ranch owner agreed to lower their rent in exchange for James attending to some daily chores on the ranch.

Fred and Dolly were married that same summer and moved to the Walker Lake country where Fred was hired to manage a ranch. Three months before, Elmer married his lady bronc rider, and they were living in California. The hell-raising days of the 111's were now just a memory.

James stayed close to the ranch and his work. Except for Sunday visits and dinners at the Conradt's, he had little interest in going other places. But for weeks he was restless, not as a *fiddlefoot*, but in his mind. He had all the energy to succeed and to make great strides as a western illustrator. But these aspirations, while anxious ones for James, were clumsy as a pup trying to move about. Something was missing. While aware that he would not be an artist as great as Russell, James intensely desired to create some artistic presentation of the western theme. In early fall, and somewhat suddenly, but with perfect harmony to his sketching, James began to write. Alice had frequently prodded James to write during their marriage. To her, writing seemed simple and logical for James since she knew he told stories without effort, interestingly and with a colorful choice of language. James had shunned the idea whenever Alice had lately made the suggestion to him, not with a definite refusal, but with a shrug of his shoulders that suggested either a future possibility or a momentary lack of interest.

When Alice mentioned the idea again, it caught James' interest. In his discussions with her, he was doubtful, however, of an ability to write the way editors would want, in proper English and "all that sort of learnin'. Besides," he went on to say, "If *Life* turned down those sketches, what you think they'll do to something I'd write?"

Alice countered James' argument with his bias about unauthentic western stories, and at least his language and writing would be of the real cowboy. She even suggested he write a story about bucking horses since that was all he ever seemed to talk about.

A week later James showed Alice an article, written in longhand and with a dozen illustrations. He titled the article, "Bucking Horses and Bucking Horse Riders." The words had flowed easily for him, and he wrote it just as if he were seated on his haunches with some buckeroos at a cow camp and telling his stories. He told Alice it was, "too easy done to be any good."

Nonetheless, James sent the article to *Scribner's Magazine* with all expectations it would be returned to him. For days afterwards, Alice also became apprehensive, not about the article, but what its rejection could do to James. He tried to cover any concern for his article, and when Alice would go for the mail, she sensed how he tensed himself in expectation of seeing the envelope he had addressed to himself when he submitted the story. She wished James had not banked his entire hopes on that one story. And there were moments when she felt maybe she should not have encouraged him so persistently to write. Great expectations have, as a lurking shadow, great disappointments, and she worried that the return of the article might cower James from any further writing and possibly dismantle what he had so far built with his art.

For James, doubt eddied in his mind because he saw in his work no similarity to what was currently finding its way in print. Other writers and illustrators of the west were different from James' style and in this difference he saw less than best in his own work. He failed to realize that this difference, rather than being mediocre, was actually a superior piece of regional literature. True art, like true writing, is personal, and no two pieces of work should ever be alike.

Scribner's Magazine accepted James' first article and paid him three hundred dollars. For two days James could hardly believe that something he had written was to be published by an "eastern outfit" and he constantly re-read the letter of acceptance. His confidence and ambition soared, and he immediately set himself to writing other articles in hours-long sessions. Frequently he wrote and sketched until dawn.

In their acceptance letter, *Scribners* asked James to write a short preface about himself, which was to accompany his article. The preface James wrote is a pedantic defense of the article; a very direct notice that he was a real cowboy who lived the cowboy life extensively, as few others have.

Without straining a brain cell, a reader could sense that the article was written by a cowboy and not some scholar of western life. James' written language makes that obvious. Even more, the deep sensitivity in the way the story is told also assures the reader that its author lived the experiences. James, however, did not realize how well he had told his story. Maybe he wrote the bragging preface to pinpoint exactly the authenticity of his story and his written language in comparison to the western trash he so despised. Or maybe, he was over-compensating — propping the walls of deep insecurity about his self-styled life he described as his own.

"Bucking Horses and Bucking Horse Riders" is an expression of western horses and the men that tame and ride them. It qualifies as one of James' best writings by carrying with it a strong and truthful scent of western life. As with most of James' early writings, these have the blood of life circulating through them and they are, consequently, good history and good literature of the cow country. While James continued to communicate what was basically true, he wrote convincingly. But as most critics who know the west will tell, James ran dry of elemental truths in his writings and sketching, and leaned to histrionics.

For the moment, however, his energy to write drew its thoughts from roots that were soaked with nostalgia and a feeling for the earth, its people and a culture which had been made by the land, sky and livestock. James plunged deep into the inkwell, and in longhand wrote a series of stories about the manners and mores of the cowboy. "A Cowpuncher Speaks," a mirroring about the western country, the way it had been before social and economic upheavals, gives a strong feeling of James' sentiment for the open range days. *Scribner's Magazine* accepted this story, while the *Saturday Evening Post* purchased "Piñon and the Wild Ones," an excellent account of wild horse trapping. *Sunset* let James know they were feeling neglected, and James sold them a three-part article called, "Bronc Twisters." With these same stories, James also produced some of his best illustrating.

Suddenly, his past and somewhat financially barren life, changed to abundance. James was paying what debts he owed, and now had money in his pocket and in the bank. It was an opportune time for him to buy his first car. He and Alice went to a Reno dealer and, after some initial pricing, decided to purchase a 1920 Pierce Arrow. "That's the one," he told Alice, and as she was to learn, he always picked the biggest car to buy. The salesman asked James if he wanted any instructions to drive the car. James said he did not. Alice had never seen James drive a car before but assumed he knew what he was doing. James found reverse, backed out of the garage like a bronc coming out of a chute, and hit a telephone pole on the other side of the street. He stood up on the car seat and yelled to Alice, still in the garage driveway, "I spurred it too hard!" A week later the repaired car was delivered to James at the Coughlin Ranch.

Scribner's Magazine bought two more articles: "Cattle Rustlers" and "Cowboys North and South." *Sunset* accepted "Desert Range Riding" and was also paying $300 an article. It wasn't too difficult to save some money and once his bank account looked promising, James suggested to Alice that it would be nice to have that place of their own with a few horses and a studio. There was a piece of land he had looked at between Reno and Carson City, at Franktown in Washoe Valley, that completely suited him.

Washoe Valley is one of the more beautiful areas in western Nevada. From the Sierra mountains, the land glides gently down to level pastures and then to desert growth where it meets and rises gradually to brown tinted hills in the east. On the Sierra side of the valley, thick with pines, James purchased five acres. It afforded a panoramic view of the valley and a clear sight to Washoe Lake on the eastern side of the valley.

James desired only a cabin and went to Alice's father for advice on materials and building. To his surprise, Alice's father and two brothers, Bill and Ed, said they would build the cabin for him and Alice.

It was a four-room cabin with a large fireplace in the parlor. An especially large window was installed to allow a broad, clear sight into the valley. On the eastern side of the house, corrals were built for the three horses which James had bought. Adjacent to the corrals were set the small barn and tack room. Above the house, and where the pines were thick, James built his studio, a log sanctuary just large enough for his writing desk and art materials.

He now had his studio, his cabin and his horses, and everything was hunky-dory. Those wistful dreams he and Alice frequently talked about were now very much real. And with these roots, he felt content and enjoyed the pleasures of his own land and his own home.

Each morning, after his breakfast, he went to the corrals and fed the horses. While they ate, James sat on the corral railing rolling his cigarettes and thinking. He enjoyed being alone, when in deep thought, and sometimes would sit there quietly and motionless for over an hour. Many times Alice watched him from the cabin as he chain-smoked, and she often wondered whatever it was that held him so deeply in thought. Then suddenly, he would hop off the railing and head for his studio. James left definite instructions for Alice that he was never to be disturbed while he was in his studio; "not even by you, Alice," he told her. He would only come for lunch if he were absolutely hungry. At first, Alice would have lunch prepared for him, but later resigned herself to prepare his meals only if he appeared.

In the following months, James' accelerating career was tantamount to a fairy tale success story. He wrote nothing that did not find a willing publisher. *Scribner's* took "The Longhorns," and "Makings of a Cow Horse," and the *Post* bought, "Once a Cowboy." Calendar companies approached him for illustrating services, and *Redbook,* for a story. Western pulp magazines who once rejected James' art portfolio now asked for his illustrating services. Between writings, James worked fervently with renewed interest in oil painting and watercolor.

Although James would not think of the title for some years yet, he was already *The Lone Cowboy,* much to Alice's dismay. In some ways she was still youthfully oriented with romantic idealism about marriage. But on the other hand, James was hardly *Prince Charming.* Sometimes Alice would not see James for an entire day and night. Often he would arise before she did, and not come back from his studio until early next morning. She drifted into lonely wanderings around the ranch or went horseback riding on the trails behind the cabin. For a while, she blamed herself for not having some of James' attentions, but soon realized that he was just not the ideal husband. He withdrew too excessively within himself and his work.

Yet, Alice was intelligent and emphatic enough to realize that she had married a talented man, and some exceptions to conventional behavior were to be expected of him. She felt that in time he would accept his writing as a job with only so many hours to be devoted to it. She waited anxiously for this sensible adjustment to his success.

Alice had wanted a child soon after their marriage. James reasonably felt that they could not afford the expense and responsibility. With James now making steady sales and to all indications, a success, she revived the thought. Again James expressed disfavor. Alice vowed she would not ask him again, and was more convinced than ever that James should not have married. He exhibited too much selfishness, not with material things, as he often bought her presents, but within himself, and for his work. With his first articles, he frequently sought Alice's advice about a sentence structure, spelling or other story ideas. Now he never consulted her, and she never knew what he had written until it appeared in print. Once after reading one of his articles, Alice offered what she believed to be a constructive criticism. He became resentful and down-graded her suggestions since the editor, he said, had felt it good enough to be accepted.

Fred and Dolly visited frequently on week-ends. Not often would James interrupt an entire writing day for them, and usually excused himself for at least a morning of work. In the afternoons and early evenings they socialized and took horseback rides. One week-end, James mentioned a foreman's job that was open on the Elsman property next to James', and how nice it would be if Fred and Dolly lived close by. They thought so too. James introduced Fred to Mr. Elsman and, within an hour, Fred accepted the position. The foursome spent considerable time together and the few years they were to live near each other would nurture a deep attachment.

By spring of 1924, James had a considerable number of manuscripts in the *Scribner's* office and they informed him that his articles, including those published in *Sunset,* would be published in book form.

It was in October of 1924 that *Cowboys North and Sout..* appeared. James had good reason to be proud of the book for the critics themselves uttered the praise that James wanted to hear. *The Times* of London suggested that the sketches of the artist, Will James, "had nothing to fear from comparison with the work of Frederick Remington or any other artist of the plains."[1]

The New York Times book reviewer was also complimentary but with keener observations:

> "Let the skeptic reader be assured at the start that the book makes excellent reading in spite of its handicap of truth. The author evidently combines keen logical insight with a rich sense of romance. While confining himself to facts, the facts he brings forward are by no means dry . . ."[2]

Wide acceptance of an author's first book is as phenomenal as it is pleasing to the publisher, and *Scribner's* immediately saw in Will James the sort of writer whose name and style could sell books. Maxwell Perkins, one of *Scribner's* astute editors, wrote James a suggestion for developing his naturalistic writing style.[3]

Dec. 5, 1924.

Dear Mr. James.

I suppose you have seen enough reviews of "Cowboys North and South" to know with what enthusiasm the critics and literary observers have received it, and as much on account of the text as the pictures. I enclose a review that has just come from Struthers Burt; but the comments of the ordinary unliterary citizen, who is really the important critic in the end, would probably interest you more, and, if so, those I heard would please you much. As for the sale, it goes well and promises to go better.

Anyway, the outcome of the publication has already been such, it seems to us, as to give you any assurance you may have wanted of marked success in book writing; I hardly think you could have had any doubts at all upon the matter of illustrating. I am therefore writing to suggest that you

[1]*The Times,* London, November 20, 1924.
[2]*New York Times,* October 12, 1924.
[3]*Editor to Author;* The Letters of Maxwell E. Perkins. Charles Scribner's Sons, 1950.

consider following this book with another, written in the
same manner but different in design, a continuous narrative
with as much or as little plot as you thought best, which
would bring into the compass of a single story the adventures
and incidents characteristic of a young cowboy's career, related in his own words. Really the book I have in mind —
for unsatisfactory as comparisons are, one can never altogether avoid them — is "Huckleberry Finn." There was very
little plot to it, you probably remember. Its great interest
was simply in the incidents and scenes of the trip on a raft
down the Mississippi, told in the language of a boy. Of
course, "Huckleberry Finn" is primarily a boy's book and it
would be better if what you would do were not altogether
that, but the great thing is that any such consecutive narrative would give your unquestionable talent for graphic
human writing a chance beyond that which this book gave.
And we suspect that it would show an equal skill in making
types and characters realizable as individuals. Won't you
consider this? We should then have a book of novel size,
to sell as a novel, and would be quite justified in having
great expectations for it. We, of course, see it also as illustrated with your own pictures. I have talked to Mr. Chapin[1]
about this and he is in hearty accord with the plan.

Cowboys North and South is James' best non-fiction work. Since
Smoky must remain fiction in spite of James' claims of the book
being true, *Cowboys North and South* displays James as a
graphic and emotionally involved writer. But instead of improving with successive books, James' writing declines. This is not
noticeable at first, but in retrospect, one can detect where sincerity and a very real devotion pervades his first book, which
is made up of his first written articles. From then on, James slowly
reverts to rehashing and masquerading his stories told in first
person.

Logically, if his first stories are better than his later efforts,
it is because in those first stories he was communicating his truth.

[1]Joseph Hawley Chapin, at the time, head of Scribner's Art Department.

They burn brighter because of his personal participation. But when his real truth ran dry, and commercialism became his path, James, probably without actually realizing it, turned to half-truths and a burlesque presentation of the cowboy and the west.

But with *Cowboys North and South* (and a few of his other books), James provides a literary pleasure for his reader; an unfiltered look at the last horseman of the range in the last decade in the age of horse culture. In "Bucking Horses and Bucking Horse Riders," which is included in the book, James shows eloquently what is real to him. To the eastern reader especially, a bucking horse is a bucking horse. When James wrote of the broncs, however, he has his reader experience the convulsive scene of the twists, grunts and tricks of the bucking horse and the pounding the rider takes while aboard. In the article, "Cowboys North and South," the lead story in the book, James tells of a range country knowledge that has all but been forgotten today. He describes a time when distinct regions of cowboy customs, equipment, hat styles, horses, and round-up procedures showed differently in the Spanish-influenced cow country of the Far West, the buckaroo country of the Northwest and the Texas way. James lived the cowboy life during the tail end of those regional distinctions, and before Hollywood, circuit rodeos and mass saddle production eclipsed local artisans and made *cowboy* the singular name of all range riders who now saddle and dress very much alike.

"Winter Months in a Cow Camp," is a pleasant reflection of isolation and cattle chores in snowbound cow country, and the *whoop-it-up* joy with the coming of spring. Wild horse round-ups, before chasing in flatbed trucks and planes, are well told in "Piñon and the Wild Ones."

Since the entire book is the essence of truth, a very passionate and personal truth of James', *Cowboys, North and South* is literary. It alone could have assured James a select place in the bookshelves of the west. As he went on, however, he lost the soul-rending believability in his stories. He would be away too long from the cow camp fraternity, where he could feel the dismalness of rain and mud...the sense of comradeship, and the patient knowledge that soon the sun would shine. This was the source of his first inspirations, and as its reality faded from his feelings, he became like many of the proverbial *old timers* who told exaggerated stories so often they actually believed them themselves.

Most of James' future writings, especially those in the first person, are pipe-dreams; over-processed thoughts that James honestly believed were true. They were intense, all-conquering of his personality and they made him evasive and difficult to understand by those who knew him. James would become an enigma to Alice, Fred, Dolly and others. But more, he was to be a perfect enigma because he would lose sense of his own perspective.

Chapter Nine

THE SUBJECTIVE sensations of a man reflect his outward actions. And if the latter appear remote to understanding, it is the
more reason that the subjective cries for empathy and not criticisms of the objective. But James allowed no one to pry deeply
or to question him as to "what is wrong," when he was sullen,
enigmatic, and a loner. He would confide with no one, and alone
bore the brunt of whatever it was that bothered him. Periodically,
he took on the appearance of a completely sad man, dejected
and forsaken looking.

Some people refused James' friendship when he was that way
and did not hesitate to tell him that they thought he was poorly
mannered. James wasn't particularly upset by those who refused
to accept him as he was. Those close to him, however, would
have to overlook many times his almost arrogant sense of independence, his moodiness, and his impatience with those who
tried to force their help upon him. They had long ago learned
not to try and "figure Bill James out..." What remained for
Alice and his friends to offer was sympathy, patience and toler-
ance; a compromise with themselves, simply because James was
easy to like. He had an intrinsic quality about him that either
made one like him in spite of his faults or dislike him completely.

During James' days of tramping, some of his fellow cowboys
found immediate fault with him, but still found room in their

opinions for admiration. Oddly, both the admiration and the
scorn sprang from a single trait of James — his ability to tell
stories. He told them with stylish believability. But some of the
cowboys recognized James' tales as "fairly tall." One cowboy
acquaintance of James' described him in the pungent but descriptive way of the cowboy . . . "We used to call him Bullshit Bill,
among ourselves. We didn't criticize him though . . . he believed
too much what he was saying for any of us to contradict him . . ."

One aspect to some understanding of the James personality
was his denial of the cow country of his time. Frequently he
had boasted, verbally and in print, that he was not a cowboy
of the 1922 variety. James referred to the total change in the
range country, the modern cowboy way of life and to dudes.
His contemptuous ridicule of that cowboy era is an interesting
piece of scorn which reveals a psychological complex.

It is more than casually evident from James' books that he
adored the west of the open range days, when a man could ride
from the Powder River in Oregon to the Powder River of Wyoming with never a fence in sight to force a detour. He liked to recall
that there was a difference among the cowhands, the cowpunch-
ers and the buckaroos — men of similar molds and cattle-made
— but divergent in their dress, saddle equipment, mannerisms of
stock handling, and each representing regional customs in the
cow country. Primarily, James describes himself as a rider of the
open range days; before the range had been fenced, before the
cowboy had to do such farming chores as putting out salt for the
cattle, riding fence with staples and plyers, and before the times
when a rider had to leave his horse to do any chores except branding. No doubt vestiges of the open range days remained in parts
of Nevada and Montana while James rode that country. But to the
degree and the style described by James with his personal pro-
noun, it was unlikely. By the time James was born, let alone
actually riding through the cow country, the range days of his

romantic mind had been closed. And more, he grew up in the times when cowboys, in name and style, were becoming more of a myth painted with a broad brush by writers, scenarists for the silent motion picture art, and ham actors in *Wild West Shows*. Real riders of the open range days were "stove up" by the time James was riding the country (from about 1910-1919). The nature of ranch and cattle work had been under economic change, and cowboys were pitching hay and learning about plowing and irrigating as range cow handling became less and less the basic economic principle of management. James' generation came after the era of the open range rider, in the twilight end of which Charlie Russell lived his western experiences. Still, James seemingly had no trouble reminiscing with Russell about the "good old days," when they got together for a talk.

Nonetheless, it was the old west — the open range that lasted until about 1890 (1910 as the widest latitude), that James loved. He talked and wrote about the country "as it was then," and in light of evidence brought out further on, much of James' wanderings about the country were very likely in search of this open range he harbored in his thoughts.

Often James exhibited active reminders of the old ways. While working for the Springer Ranch in Santa Fe, he carried an iron cinch ring tied to his saddle strings, and would use this iron ring to run the CS brand on a calf. It was an old range custom, but it had died out in that part of the country some years before.

Dick Dickson, a collector of old western artifacts at his ranch in Palm Springs, stated that James never went horseback riding with him or guests of Dickson's at a ranch get-together. James preferred to casually walk about the ranch to examine Dickson's collection. And on James' ranch in Montana, he exercised many of his desires to have the past brought back to life, or at least, to hold onto those ways that were being supplanted by newer techniques.

James was not completely overpowered by his sentimentality, and certainly not to the point of some sort of senility. It was, however, a powerful force within him, and sufficient to alter his personality at times and account for his enigmatic habits.

After the release of *Cowboys North and South,* James settled to a less rigorous writing routine. For the moment he had caught up with what he wanted to say, and now gave more of himself and his time to Alice. For her the next few years became easier than the previous four years of her marriage — which were a period of serious adjustment for her.

Alice accepted James' inexplicable mannerisms, and realized that he was not pliable to her formula for a husband. Still, life was fast-paced. What seemed dreams only yesterday for them, when they talked of log cabins, horses and a studio, already had become a reality. James' *belles-lettres* of the range were bringing him many recognitions, and at rodeos, or gatherings to sign autographs to his book, he was introduced as the *west's best cowboy artist.* While their circle of friends was limited, there was a close friendship with those they enjoyed knowing, especially Fred and Dolly. They traveled to rodeos and horse shows on weekends, and as often, stayed in the Washoe Valley for picnics and horseback riding in the mountains. Frequently Alice's family visited on the weekends. For Alice, this pattern of life in the Washoe Valley was becoming comfortable.

Even while this pattern was settling, James was starting to hint about a move. Nevada, he claimed, was beginning to crowd him and he wanted to go where there weren't any fences, and where cattle were still worked on the open range. Alice asked where, and James answered, "My birth state, Montana." Alice didn't like the idea. It meant an upheaval; leaving her family, and generally upsetting everything that had now come to seem a pleasant way of life. James detected that Alice did not share even a particle of his enthusiasm to move on to new country.

Finally, he said it was mostly a thought... "to throw a ketch rope on some other time."

His output of articles continued at a prodigious pace. *Scribner's* was receiving most of his stories, since they planned to publish another book of his articles. To *Sunset,* James fulfilled a contract to have two more articles for them by the year's end in 1924 by sending "First Money" and "When Wages are Low." Neither article is outstanding, and it is possible that James was rushing his stories at this time for he had hinted to Alice, with the non-committal grin he used when throwing out a *little bait,* that he was working on a lengthy horse story about his "Ole Smoky horse;" the story idea Maxwell Perkins had suggested in his letter.

Alice readily became aware that James was becoming more and more excited about the horse story he was writing. In his small studio in the pines, James worked in long bursts of seclusion, detached from Alice, Fred, Dolly and literally the outside world. Still, when he did emerge from his isolation, he was happy and smiling. Instead of the long writing sessions having fatigued him, he seemed only more enthusiastic. To neither Alice, Fred or Dolly had he ever talked much about what he was currently doing, but from sense of pride, he discussed somewhat the horse story he was now writing.

James labored on *Smoky* and its illustrations for almost a year while sandwiching in other articles for *Scribner's Magazine,* and one relating to his work in the movies for the *Southwest Review.* He called this one "Filling in the Cracks."

In December, 1925, the Scribner's house published the second volume of James' articles under the title *The Drifting Cowboy.* Although in retrospect, it is not as good as *Cowboys North and South,* it was still critically elevated to the same compliments that greeted his first book. As in both books, it is James' illustrations that are most favorably noted... "... as vigorously alive as a young bronc on a frosty morning . . ." commented the *Book-man*.[1] Lawrence Stallings in *Outlook* wrote: ". . . Will James has a distinct literary style. He has that and more and the Scribners have had the good judgment not to translate the book into English . . ."[2]

By April of 1926, *Scribner's Magazine* published the first of four lengthy installments of "Smoky, the One Man Horse." The cover of the magazine heralded the equine hero with a water-color done by James, and featuring Smoky and his one master, Clint. *Smoky* appeared in book form in September, 1926, with 43 full page text halftone illustrations. It drew the best reviews James was ever to read about his books. William Hornaday called it . . . "one of the truly great horse stories in our language!" The *New York Times* in a simple but high reaching compliment, said, "Will James has done the 'Black Beauty' of the cow country . . ."[3]

Smoky went into a second printing in September, another in October, twice in November, and five times in December, and has never been out of print since. The epic horse story is James' best fiction and its illustrations are his best single group of draw-ings. James missed nothing in describing the life of the range horse. The first two chapters, where James describes Smoky as a wild range colt, are a clear evidence of his keen observation and his love for horses. *Smoky* reverberates with realism, and is the essence of James' talents at its best, a true indicator of a way of life he did know — the cow country just before and after the First World War.

Smoky was a real horse. How real are all the adventures James claims with the horse in *Lone Cowboy*, *Horses I Have Known* and in *Smoky*, is again one of those uncertain areas in James' storytelling in the first person.

[1]*Bookman*, January, 1926.
[2]*Outlook*, November 25, 1925.
[3]*New York Times*, Book Section, October 10 ,1926.

James was riding a large blue roan stallion that he called Smoky when he rode into the eastern Nevada country around 1913. Riding with him was a saddle pal named Fred Allen, a tough, heavy drinking cowboy who rode a horse similar to Smoky. Both horses were the only ones of their kind in that part of the country, and it appeared they had probably been raised at the same ranch and sired by the same stallion.

Only James was capable of riding Smoky. He had won bets from other cowboys who vowed they could ride the horse, which James had encouraged by claiming that Smoky was a one-man horse. Apparently no one could ride Smoky unless they understood his bucking pattern. Smoky would buck with James too, and without provocation, but James knew the routine Smoky followed, and was able to stay aboard.

In James' years of storytelling in reference to Smoky, inconsistencies crop up. In *Lone Cowboy*, where he tells a poignant story of the horse and himself, James wrote ... "instead of the horse (Smoky) being a company horse he was my own ..."[4] Years later he wrote in *Horses I Have Known*, "Smoky wasn't my own horse. I only broke him for the outfit I was riding for at the time ..."[5]

And going further about the horse which also demonstrates James' usual inclination to be evasive, he plays a nonsensical game with his readers in telling where Smoky was born:

"Mentioning the outfit where Smoky was foaled and raised I will only say that at one time, when I was riding for it, it had cow camps and headquarters spreading in most every western state from Mexico to Canada ...

"For an identifying clue, that widespread outfit about lost all their cattle, many, many thousands in one year, and went to raising horses ..."[6]

[4]p. 178.
[5]p. 273.
[6]*Ibid.*

Will James

Most likely James was hinting of the Miller-Lux Company. More interesting, however, is his attitude. Seemingly it may appear insignificant, but basically it typifies James when (rarely) he spoke about himself to others. His statements were vague, and often teasingly generalized.

Chapter Ten

CRITICAL and public reception of *Smoky* vaulted James to a greater measure of recognition than he had ever expected. Autograph parties took him to Reno, San Francisco, Denver and New York where he also conferred with Scribners on future books.

Financial returns from *Smoky* were pleasing too, and perked up James' hopes of moving to Montana. But his dream enlarged to a cow ranch of his own in a country that had not been torn by fences.

He slipped the ketch rope off that thought he had expressed to Alice some months before, and told her specifically of land on an Indian reservation, near Billings. It suggested isolation to Alice, but a ranch of their own also carried pleasant thoughts and the wide open spaces for which James pined. She agreed to move, as did Fred, whom James wanted as foreman of the ranch. Except for Elmer, who died suddenly only weeks before, the old pact of the 111's was becoming a reality. Picking Fred to manage the ranch, however, was not merely to satisfy James' promise. Fred had considerable experience managing a cow and calf operation, and since James was admittedly "damn lazy," other than when he had to write and draw, he needed someone dependable. Fred was never to falter either, even when he was to be torn between loyalty to James and concern for his sister, Alice.

Selling their property in the Washoe Valley was unexpectedly easy. There was a neighbor at that time, a radical sanitarian, who had complained to James on several occasions that James' horses were causing a fly problem. At another time he complained that the garbage was breeding flies, which were spreading to his home.

After James and Alice had decided to move to Montana the neighbor visited again to lodge a complaint. James met the gentleman on the front porch and rolled a cigarette as the neighbor instructed James on the proper disposal of waste to curtail breeding areas for insects. When he had finished, James quietly told his neighbor that he would not have to worry any longer about garbage, bugs and horse manure. "I'll be movin' shortly," said James. "Expect to sell out to a pig farmer."

The visitor sat speechless for a disturbing moment.

"Pig farmer?" he ascertained.

"Pig farmer," drawled James.

"Has he bought yet?"

"Nope," replied James.

"I'll buy."

For years after, James delighted in telling the story of how he sold his Nevada property, and with a lot of thanks to a pig farmer that never existed.

Montana was a benediction for James' whims of the great outdoors and the great west. Essentially it had been tamed, but still the breath of mountain men and trappers lingered in the mountain country. And Billings had the aura of when it was an active cattle center and cowpuncher town. James had found an enchantment with Montana when he rode that country as a cowboy, and he always talked about the Montana country. He liked best the Crow Indian Reservation lands in southeast Montana, around Pryor, and forty-five miles south of Billings. It was a land very much alone to itself; unfenced, and about the size of the state of New Jersey. About fifteen hundred Crow Indians spread thinly across the reservation. Some of the Indians had made modest success on their land as ranchers, while others were content to lease their land to the white man.

James purchased some dead-Indian land — which was land subject to sale because no heirs had made claim. His initial purchase was about 4,000 acres and over the years, with additional leases, the ranch increased to 8,000 acres.

He selected for the home ranch a valley almost completely surrounded by red sandstone cliffs, in the foothills of the Pryor Mountains.

While James and Fred searched about the area, designating building and corral locations, James told Fred how thousands of buffalo used to roam here, and where bands of wild horses were less than two hours' horseback ride away. On the other side of the reservation was Custer Battlefield where remnants of the 7th Cavalry were duly outwitted by the Sioux and Cheyenne. It was an area where James often frequented and he liked to sit on the high cliffs where Major Reno and his men had retreated after the Indians had chased them across the Little Big Horn River.

After selecting building locations, and finishing some business transactions, James returned to Nevada, leaving Fred to start erecting the buildings with hired labor. When James returned to the Washoe Valley, Alice had already packed and arranged for the furniture shipment to Billings. Dolly had moved in with her family in Reno and was to wait there until Fred had built their home on the ranch.

The evening before James and Alice were to leave for Billings, James complained of pains in his side. By morning they were intense and Alice drove him to a Reno hospital where he was operated on for acute appendicitis. Impatiently, James remained in the hospital while Alice vacated their Washoe Valley home and stayed with her parents in Reno.

About April 1927, James was released from the hospital and with Alice, went directly to Billings. They rented a hotel room and expected to be there only about a week. James went to the ranch each day and soon became discouraged at the slow progress in building. Two weeks later, it was apparent that he and Alice could not stay at the hotel without considerable expense. Fred and his crew were living in army surplus tents. James purchased one for himself and Alice and pitched it close to where their home was being built.

While Fred supervised the labor and the building, James made spasmodic efforts to write. But it became difficult to concentrate with all the hammering noises. Each morning, after a talk with Fred, James took his writing pad and climbed to one of the bluffs overlooking the building activity.

One morning Alice suggested to James that he could give Fred a hand now and then to speed completion of their house so James could get to his full schedule of writing. James answered, "I got to make money to keep us going."

Probably no one but James realized how true that was. The land, its buildings, corrals, labor and the stock he was ready to purchase, had sunk him in a deep well of debt. To climb out required a regular flow of writing. Although James had so far held to a traditional respect in his writings about life in the west, his debts and obligations and his future plans for the ranch forced him to bend that respect. He was writing his articles quickly now, and was playing up, though not with exaggeration, the Wild West motif. Alice recalls that an editor or two had suggested to James that he add this drama. In fact it was even necessary, they insisted, since popular markets are not entirely oriented to pure truth. James made a protest to one editor, but was told that their magazine was not interested in James' iconoclastic crusade. James was in no position to argue the matter. He continued writing a flood of articles, some of which he gave the *tall yarn*.

While still in Nevada, he had started a series of articles for *Scribner's Magazine* titled, "All In A Day's Riding," and which would continue periodically into the early part of 1930. The *Saturday Evening Post* published "On Circle," "Remuda," and "Round-Up Wagon," and had a stock of articles that would cover their pages until 1928. While the *Post* and *Scribner's* became the more prolific publishers of James' writings, *Youths' Companion* was happy to receive some contributions, and *Ladies' Home Journal* assigned him illustrating work for stories they published with a western theme.

By August the ranch was finished, and alive with stock. Fred went to Reno to gather his household goods. He returned with Dolly in time to celebrate with James and Alice a telegram from Scribner's notifying James that *Smoky* had won the Newberry Award presented by the American Library Association for outstanding literature for children. Sales of the book jumped again, and Scribner's prepared to issue *Smoky* in the illustrated classic edition for which James was to add color illustrations.

Smoky did not win the award without protest from some quarters, as James was later told. That the story itself was good was not denied, but objections were lodged against the cowboy vernacular.

The point was well-taken. Words such as *wrangler, remuda, stud* and *filly*, the bad grammar, the spelling of creature as *crethure*, and the slang expressions, all seemed at first logical objections to the book. Yet, what can be considered academically as bad grammar is actually only part of what is really a consummate art that James has woven to tell his story of a horse. But in any case, time has proven the objections to be void in view of the many other qualities that *Smoky* offers. Well-written myths of the west were worse to some critics than truths written in vernacular that, in spite of bad grammar, had at least an essence of truth. *Smoky* is literature.

There is a certainty in characterization and a skillful portrayal of Smoky that does not become a slobbering tale of an unfortunate horse whose feelings are propped with a lot of humanizing. And if such verbs as *figgered* or *sashayed* cause a shudder, then there is a self-cheating of an interesting and true range language with concise, meaningful and straight-from-the-shoulder expressions.

Chapter Eleven

JAMES called his ranch, the *Rocking R* and it became the embodiment of what James hoped would resemble the old west. He wasn't too concerned with some of the newer agricultural developments that had come upon the scene, or some of the more rapid methods of handling cattle through corrals and chutes. "Rope 'em and brand 'em like the old-timers," he instructed the cowboys hired during round-up.

Both privately and publicly James confirmed that he wanted to "keep alive what was passing in the west." and wanted things around "that reminded me of the old west."[1] At times Fred became annoyed with this singular emphasis by James, but with some empathy nonetheless, told Dolly, "If that's the way Bill wants it, I guess I can understand his mood." While Fred developed the ranch into a cow and calf operation, James dabbled in aesthetic whims.

One of the first images James retained about the west was the longhorn cattle. He had a small herd of Mexican longhorns shipped to his ranch from Oklahoma and they became his favorite conversation theme to ranch visitors. To friends and guests, James liked to demonstarate how the beef animal had changed, and he would compare the longhorn with the old-time cowman, both of which, he said with a personal boast, were tough and

[1]Newspaper clippings; no date, in Billings Public Library.

independent. The newer cattle breeds, he would add, like the new cowboys, were pasture fattened.

James allowed no hunting on his ranch. To him the grace and beauty of deer, antelope, elk and the big cats, meant more than just game to be stalked and killed. He acquired a pet deer which roamed the ranch at will, along with dogs, pet rabbits and cats, of which he and Alice were especially fond. Later, he had a pond developed and stocked it with Canadian geese so he could "watch them fly."

James did not permit the main road to his ranch to be paved. Rains caused gullies, and the washboard patterns became standard jokes in Billings. The "James kidney rocker" it was called. But that was why he liked that part of the country, he told a Billings newspaper, "because it has poor roads."[2]

Alice had kept busy furnishing the main house, and traveling with James to rodeos and dinner socials. She no longer became as distressed by James' periods of isolation with his work or his lack of conversation at the dinner table when he was deep in thought.

James was not entirely aloof to Alice when he was attentive to his work. Often at a low ebb of her loneliness, James would surprise her with a gift. A new horse or a saddle, a trip to New York or San Francisco where James had to meet with his publisher or to make a lecture tour, always seemed to emerge when she needed that lift. Shortly after settling in Montana, James told Alice one morning, "Your folks will be here in a couple of hours. Better get yourself to Billings to meet 'em."

Like all his surprises for Alice, pleasant or frightening, he would spring them on her when she least expected. James had wired train fare to her parents, together with an open invitation to stay at the ranch as long as they wished.

When Alice's parents made their first visit to the ranch, her

[2]*Ibid.*

father confided to Alice that he had certainly been wrong about James. He was happy that James had done well for himself and for Alice, and apologized to her for his mulish attitude against her marrying James. But Alice's father was never to know how his first thoughts about James being a "sly cowboy" and not suitable for Alice, were a correct sizing. For years Alice would never talk about her troubles with James, or his perplexing and contradictory ways, not even to Dolly. Only after the death of Alice's father did she talk extensively to her mother of her strained relationship with James. There wasn't any particular time that Alice can lift up as a date when the frictional wedge came between her and James. To start with, she had married a man she knew only superficially. But at that time they shared dreams and aspirations, and this can override other uncertain facets of human relations. Once recognition was attained by James, rapport between him and Alice seemed to shrink. After their move to Montana, and until they separated in 1935, their life together was eight years of generating turbulence. Arguments about James' heavy drinking; his disappearing without notice of departure or destination, and money talks — large sums of money that James could not or would not account for — brought out from both of them a dizzy array of words that never revealed answers.

Success, which had been the prize James reached for, began to turn on him. He was slow to adjust to change, and success came too quickly, and with such continued rapidity to allow no mutual or even momentary meeting of the minds between him and Alice. Parties grew in intensity when movie stars, publishers or other dignitaries stopped at the Rocking R to visit. James would drink to excess, and would start telling stories that were inconsistent with what he had previously told Alice years earlier. At first Alice would question him about what he had said, (usually it was a story about his days with Bopy), and

James would become evasive, and suggest she must have heard him wrong.

Alice frequently sensed she was fighting some invisible force in James that determined his actions and reactions and which, seemingly, had no motive. Often she had been accused of not understanding James, and was told she was to expect a certain amount of capricious behavior from him. After all, he was an artist, and at those times he was creative. But these whimsical tangents no longer bothered Alice. What did confuse her was his moody disposition that did not yield into creativity, but instead, turned into nasty insults. At moments when she virtually screamed at him to tell her what was bothering him, he offered an excuse too trivial to be the cause of his vagaries. Alice knew he was lying. James, aware that she sensed his insincerity, frequently disappeared. Two, three days later, he would return, and go back to his studio without excuse or apology.

When the emotional disturbances did subside, and James had better control of himself and what was bothering him, he was as most people knew him, kind, gentle, tolerant though rarely indulgent, and sociable. Most of all, after one of his emotional eruptions, he was gentle with Alice, and this would cast a glimmer of hope for her that their marriage could last.

Cow Country, James' third book, was another assemblage of his short stories. It appeared in October 1927. Like its predecessors, it received high admiration from the critics. One of the stories in particular, *Complete,* is almost biographical of James' nostalgic and restless nature.

Similar to James, the story's hero is "Dude" Douglas, a cowboy who has tired of drifting. James introduces "Dude" as he is riding night guard around a bedded herd . . .

"There's many things comes to a cowboy's mind at such times; the quiet of the night, the dark shadow of the big herd, and the steady swing of the pony's gait are all, it seems like, in cahoots to bring out what might be buried the deepest in a man's think-tank. And it was as that cowboy was riding along and sort of keeping his eyes and the edge of the herd that particular night that the dark shadows of cattle and horns begin to sort of evaporate, and as what came to his mind took shape, there came visions like of a timbered hillside, then a creek with quakers and cotton-woods along it, and by them cottonwoods a rambling log house and corrals — his own log house and his own corrals."

James weaves a gentle but growing hunger about "Dude" wanting to settle down on a place of his own. "Dude" soon exchanges bucking horse work for the more gentle occupation of riding into his pastures and estimating the weight of his steers. But the rambling fever still persits, and hammers at "Dude" to follow the seasons throughout the cow country. Even as he follows this urge, he feels homesick for his spread. It is only when he finds the right gal, marries her, and returns with her to his ranch is his life and happiness complete.

The story of "Dude" is one of James' better short stories. It has the feel of the earth in the days not so long ago when earth was both a necessity and a feeling to most western men.

After his first winter on the Rocking R, James planned to stay at the ranch only during the warmer months of the year. The Montana winter had hemmed him in, and frequently it was too cold for him to sit for any length of time to write and paint. In that first winter of 1927-1928, he started a set of paintings for the classical edition of *Smoky* that Scribner's was preparing to release. He had also started another book, a horse story, he called *Sand*.

That summer James and Alice also toured the western country, and attended rodeos in Wyoming, Colorado, Utah and Arizona. He was guest announcer at a few of them, and was often interviewed by local newspapers. While touring he continued to work on *Sand* and some short stories. He sold "The Big Hat" to the

Post, and "Up In The Eagle Territory" to *Scribner's Magazine.*

It amazed Alice how he ever found time to write and illustrate while traveling. Invariably, James spent considerable time with cowboys at rodeos, and usually he would leave her in the grandstands and head for the chutes to carouse with the cowboy contestants. It became a steady diet for Alice to return to the hotel alone as James had left a message that he had "gone with the boys for a spell." James might return to the hotel by himself, but more constantly, it would be a group of cowboys returning with him drunk.

While it seems to Alice that James' heavy drinking began after his success, it was a habit that had been noted long before he ever married. His prison record in Carson City indicates this as do the recollections of those who knew him when he was riding freely throughout the Nevada country. At the time James was courting Alice, he drank only sporadically. Following his marriage, being away from cowboys, and his singular compulsion to his art and writing, squelched his alcoholic thirst to only a rare drink.

But after his success had lost its polish, he became easy prey to drinking under encouraging conditions. With free-wheeling cowboys in Hollywood, parties in New York, Palm Springs or Santa Barbara, and particularly when something was bothering him, he drank until he was in a stupor. At the ranch there was a steady parade of celebrities and other friends. The drinking parties, while enjoyable to those on the James' ranch when in moderation, became too commonplace, and stirred the conflicts between James and Alice.

Alice had berated him numerous times when he was considerably drunk, and embarrassed guests or hosts. This always precipitated an argument. Finally, James refused to take Alice with him on extended trips. Often giving her only an hour's notice, he would take the train to New York or Chicago to cover rodeos and write features for the larger metropolitan news-papers.

But in those first few years in Montana, after James decided the winters were too severe for him to accomplish his work, he and Alice would go to New York for a brief visit and then re-turn to either San Francisco or Hollywood for the season. He scheduled himself to write a book during the winter, and also in the summer when he returned to the ranch.

Usually Fred would write James and tell him, "the horses are shedding out," and it was time for him and Alice to return to the Rocking R. For about a week after, James poked around the ranch, and rode with Fred to see how the stock had wintered. After this ritual, James retreated to his studio where he would begin another book. For at least three months he was prac-tically incommunicado and only in the evenings would he join Alice, sometimes with Fred and Dolly, for supper. Usually on Sunday, he stayed away from his work to loaf about the ranch or to go into the hills.

When James would finish another book, about August or Sep-tember, he would announce to Alice, Fred and Dolly that he had, "a new one packed and on its way." Almost habitually, he would begin a three or four day inebriation; a twilight existence in which he neither seemed aware of what he said or did. Dolly remembers these episodes of James' as her most vivid memories while living on the Rocking R.

"It was frightening and pitiful. He often scared Alice. Once he took a pistol and poked it into Alice's ribs and cocked the hammer. He wasn't angry. He just thought it was funny. A few days later Fred told him what he did, and that the gun was loaded. Bill went to Alice and cried as he apologized. He just never seemed to know what he was doing when he drank."

When in such a hazy state, James was uninhibited, and the turn of a thought in his mind was quickly enacted. In New York one year he led the rodeo parade. Suddenly, he reined his horse off the street and rode into a prominent hotel and shot at the lobby lights. Texas, Hollywood and Montana also would be branded with James' cowboy capers.

In the summer of 1928, James was nearly finished with *Sand*, and Scribner's editor Whitney Darrow[3] was keeping James to a tight writing deadline. With the plans for further books outlined for James, he was able to borrow advances from Scribner's for water development on the ranch and some necessary fencing.

Although James' cash barometer would drop very low now and then, he continually bought horses unnecessarily. It annoyed Fred, since their expenses were marked against the cow operation, and often Fred reminded James that they had too many horses that were just "soaking up hay."

"We had more horses then we ever needed," remembers Dolly. "But horses were the one animal Bill wanted around the place. It made no difference whether we needed them or not, if Bill liked a certain horse, he bought him, even the drafty, work horses which Bill had special sympathy for. Many times, Bill would wander to the corrals and spend time with the draft horses. One day when I had finished milking the cow and was leading it back to pasture, I heard Bill under a lean-to speaking to the team of Percheron work horses we had. He said: 'Old-timers, they're taking away all that's good in the west. You too.'"

Dolly smiled when she heard James talking to the horses, and in looking back she remembers James as his kindest and gentlest when he was with the animals, and especially the horses.

James reflects this tendency also when he writes about animals; sharing an empathy that emerges as pure literature in some paragraphs of his writings. In an early article he titled, "A Cowpuncher Speaks," James contemplated the changes that have

[3]A vice-president at Scribner's who advised and handled James' business arrangements with the publishing house.

entered the west. His ending of the story is a sorrowful reflection which he shares with a coyote:

"As I'm setting upon this little knoll taking a last look at the country where I'd put in so many hard rides, a little coyote rambles up the side of the hill, sees me and stops, starts to run some more, then somehow feels that I'm harmless and stops again. I see him limping and notice a trap kept one of his paws. He, too, has been crowded a heap, and somehow I have more admiration for him than I used to. I'd like to let him know we're not enemies no more."

In *Piñon and the Wild Ones,* another of James' first efforts, he mourns the passing of the wild horses.

"I'm kind of sorry now so many were caught, 'cause I have a lot of respect and admiration for the mustang . . . For they really belong, not to man, but to that country of junipers and sage, of deep arroyos, mesas — and freedom."

When James writes about wild animals, he is never loquacious. There is no hint of the "tall tale." Instead, he is very honest, and his writing picturesque and melancholy. He writes lucidly and simply, and together the writing became a lively bit of literature.

Chapter Twelve

WHEN James finished *Sand,* he and Alice took the train to New York City for conferences with Scribner's. Arrangements had been made by Scribner's for James to lecture, and to autograph books, throughout the metropolitan area.

An apartment was rented on Madison Avenue, and for the first few days after their arrival in New York, James conferred with his Scribner's editor, Maxwell Perkins, about *Sand.* Some rewriting and some additional drawings were suggested for the book. James had high hopes for this book, an approach in theme that he had not attempted before. It was a romantic novel about a dude that becomes a cowboy, tames a wild stallion, and wins for himself a western heroine.

During this New York trip, James also visited the editorial offices of the *Ladies' Home Journal.* The past summer he had illustrated a Hal Borland story called "Haven," which was published by the magazine, and now they wanted James to do the drawings for a Mary Roberts Rinehart story, "Dude West," and James agreed to illustrate the story.

Alice had hopes that she and James would travel through upstate New York. James agreed to the idea, but at the time, neither was prepared for the response to James' talks and book autographing parties. Fans swarmed to the sessions to see this *exotic* individual from the west; to hear him talk in his picturesque language and curious grammar. James wore western clothes and boots, and this to the kids was like the second coming to the east of another *Buffalo Bill*. James reveled in the attention they were heaping on him at Macy's book stores and New York's horse society groups. It was particularly amazing to James the way the kids would cater to him and would ask him to tell stories and draw pictures. He always obliged them in the simple and plain cowboy talk they wanted to hear. "Someday," he told Alice, "I'm gonna write a story just for kids who want to come west and can't. I know how they feel."

Evenings were no less demanding on James' time. Parties and social affairs were frequently given in his honor. In October, the rodeo at Madison Square Garden was in session, and James presented trophies to winning cowboys. While the rodeo was in town Alice hardly saw James, and even Scribner's was curious as to where he was. Alice told Scribner's as she did others who inquired for James, that he was with the cowboys — wherever they were at the moment.

On the train coming to New York, James casually outlined to Alice another horse story he hoped to start while there. Now, after the social whirl and overnight disappearances by James with the rodeo cowboys, Alice reminded him of his new story idea. He answered that the book would have to wait until he got back to the ranch, as he hadn't the time. Alice countered by stating that there would be time if he would stop going to every party to which he was invited, and stop carousing with cowboys. James didn't agree. It would be rude to act stand-offish, he said.

By April 1929, James turned fickle again and grew tired of New York. Some of the additional sketches he was to do for *Sand* had not been started, and he told Alice that they were getting back to the ranch, where he could get something done.

Within a week after arriving at the ranch, James mailed the *Sand* sketches to New York, and immediately turned to completing the oil painting for the classical edition of *Smoky*, which was due to be published in 1929. The paintings were also scheduled for exhibit in Montana, Texas, New York and Los Angeles. Writing slowed as James absorbed himself in painting, and only one article, "The Turning Point," was sent to *Scribner's Magazine*.

Sand appeared in May, and was clobbered by the critics, who in general, considered the book far below the standard of James' best work. Van de Water in the *New York Post* was most fault-finding:

"Will James' drawings are as good as usual, but his text is deplorable. A novel, after all, demands something more than draftsmanship and a perversity in spelling. Further Mr. James' smug belief that all virtue is sequestered between the Missouri and the Rockies, irritates us a trifle."[1]

Sand is probably James' worst book, and insulting to the easterner as Van de Water adequately protested. But bad reviews rarely disconcerted James. What would raise the hackles on his neck, however, was criticism from editors or reviewers that his written language sounded phony, or needed some *Englishizing.* "No one," he stated to Alice, "was to change his writing. That was the way he talked and the way he wrote, and editors can take it or leave it."

A critic once said of James that his language was not in the cowboy vernacular. James angrily replied that his talk had been picked up and mixed from the different localities of the cow country. The language of the cowboy, as he noted, "Is just as different as the style of rigs and ways of working." James liked the cowboy tongue, and possibly he did over-use it for commercial emphasis.

While critics, as has been said, hardly upset James when they showed only lukewarm attention to his books, he nonetheless was critical of them. There was a strutting cockiness in James' atti-

[1]*New York Evening Post,* May 4, 1929.

tude about his books. He felt that since they were written by a real westerner, this in itself made them unique. Critics did realize this, and weren't bashful about heaping praise on his books when it was due James. What James failed to realize was how his writing was changing by the time *Sand* came to the public. He would recuperate to better writing after *Sand*, but a decline is nevertheless noticeable.

Most of his critics and those that knew James attributed his behavioral change and excessive drinking to his success which had come too quickly. With the greater pressures that came with his success and his troubles with Alice, he jerked back from reality and hid peacefully in drink and the past. He allowed himself a sort of hypnotism with the past whenever pressures became overflowing. He never lost his entire sense of reality, however, as he did admit that he drank too much and could be nasty when drunk.

"Good things are a lot like bad things in a way, they all come at once."

James wrote that line in *Big Enough*, but had used them first with Alice when she argued with him as to why he was doing the things that were ruining their marriage.

It seemed now, too, that small differences were twisting their entire relationship. A dance in Billings to which Alice wanted to go was without any interest for James. Alice went alone and James became furious. At other functions, he accused her of being "sweetly attentive" to other men. Alice did encourage some attentions, wanting to make James jealous and more attentive to her. It was a woman's device, as natural as applying makeup. She abandoned the skit when she saw that it enraged James instead of attracting his affectionate attentions. Alice might join in a drink, to please James, but Fred and Dolly would refrain in spite of James' ridicule of Fred for being a teetotaler.

Outside his studio on the *Rocking R*, James frequently worked
on his illustrations for his books. His horses were kept close by in
a corral where he could closely observe them and sketch ideas.

— *Courtesy of Eleanor Snook.*

ROCKING R TEPEE AND COTTAGE

The boss of the *Rocking R* spent as much time in the tepee entertaining guests as he did in his home. Often neighboring kids would ride to the James ranch to see the famous cowboy. Alice greeted these boys, one of whom took this picture.

— Courtesy of Dolly Conradt.

114

CLINT

t served as a model for James when he was illustrating the books Scribner's
preparing for young readers. The horse pictured was reserved for guests of
es who knew nothing of horses and riding. When they invariably remarked
they didn't know about horses, James used the old joke, "Well, he doesn't
vn anything about people. So both of you can start fresh together..."

— *Courtesy of Dolly Conradt.*

THE RANCH IN WINTER

ers were too severe for James to attempt any writing and illustrating. Dolly
Fred, with Clint loyally stayed on at the ranch and cared for the stock.

— *Courtesy of Dolly Conradt.*

"... with life, action and humor, which almost tears out of the page—

— *Literary Review,* November 28, 1925.

Reproduced with the permission of Charles Scribner's Sons fr
SMOKY (Copyright 1926 Charles Scribner's Sons; renewal co
right 1954 Charles Scribner's Sons and Auguste Dufault).

"...you can hear the squeal of the animal and the creak of strained leather." — *North American*, December 1927.

Reproduced with the permission of Charles Scribner's Sons from SMOKY (Copyright 1926 Charles Scribner's Sons; renewal copyright 1954 Charles Scribner's Sons and Auguste Dufault).

"The winter camp ... And the work goes on the same if the sun
is shining or a blizzard is howling."

Reproduced with the permission of Charles
Scribner's Sons from ALL IN A DAY'S RIDING
(Copyright 1933 Charles Scribner's Sons; re-
newal copyright © 1961 Auguste Dufault).

118

"The end of the season. The cowboys that are not kept on payroll catch up their private ponies and hit out with the birds..."

Reproduced with the permission of Charles Scribner's Sons from ALL IN A DAY'S RIDING (Copyright 1933 Charles Scribner's Sons; renewal copyright © 1961 Auguste Dufault).

ROPE AND HOT IRON

Reproduced with the permission of Charles Scribner's Sons from BIG ENOUGH (Copyright 1931 Charles Scribner's Sons; renewal copyright © 1959 Auguste Dufault).

120

For the first time, in late 1929, Alice wrote her mother a lengthy letter about her differences with James, and implied that unless he changed she would leave him. Her mother wired Alice immediately that James probably needed her more now than ever. Alice wasn't convinced that James needed her. She threatened to leave him unless he stopped drinking. James wrote to Mother, and pleaded with her to convince Alice not to leave. This repetitious pattern would become commonplace, with Alice finally being persuaded by her mother to stay with James.

At other times James wrote to his mother-in-law, emoting that she was the mother he never had and that she understood him better than Alice. Grievances between James and Alice were painfully felt by Alice's mother.

It is curious that neither Alice nor James ever asked for a divorce. In spite of simmering and sporadic arguments, neither suggested that solution. George Snell, James' attorney, told James that unless he did stop drinking Alice would leave him. Snell pointedly told James that he was in sympathy with Alice. James admitted to Snell that he still loved Alice. Yet, he would never say those words to her.

In November 1929, James arranged to leave for New York to see his publisher. Alice wanted to go along with him, as she hoped to hold James to moderation from his heavy drinking. He told her plainly that it wasn't necessary for her to come with him. His business would not take long, and since they planned to stay the rest of the winter in San Francisco, it would be best if she went to the west coast to locate an apartment. Alice agreed, and James promised that he would return within three weeks. This winter, he said, he wanted definitely to write that horse story which he had been mulling through his mind for nearly a year.

They said goodbye at the the Billings train station, with Alice eliciting another promise from James that he would not drink excessively and would hurry back.

Shortly after, Alice left the Rocking R and stayed in Reno for a visit with her family, and then went on to San Francisco. She found an apartment, and wired the address to James at Scribner's. James answered with a letter, and wrote that he would be finished with his conferences soon. Another letter followed, indicating his immediate departure from New York. Alice presumed James was on his way to California. After a week, and no sight of or word from James, Alice called Whitney Darrow. He told her that Bill had left New York ten days before. Alice called the hotel where James had stayed and they told her that James had checked out over a week before, and had left no forwarding address. Alice wired Fred in Montana; telephoned her mother in Reno. No one knew where James was. Alice became frantic and feared the worst, especially if James had been drinking.

Meanwhile, Whitney had done some checking on his own, and learned that James had sent a telegram to a dentist friend in San Antonio, advising of his arrival. It was Christmas Eve when Whitney telephoned Alice. She told Whitney that she had no knowledge of Bill having friends in Texas. Alice wanted to call the dentist, but Whitney admitted Bill had been drinking heavily. He felt it would be best if she went to Texas. "If he's still drinking," he told her, "it could be a whopper, and he'll need you."

Alice quickly arranged train reservations and was able to start that evening, making train connections at Los Angeles for Texas. Her mind during the entire trip was filled with premonitions that something had happened, or was going to happen to James.

After arriving at San Antonio, Alice telephoned the dentist named by Whitney. An hour later, she was still trying to contact him. Finally, she registered at a hotel, and knowing that James would not stay at anyone's home if he could stay at a dude ranch, she started calling the local dude ranches.

At the sixth ranch called, a woman proprietor admitted James was there. She wanted to see Alice first, however, and would come to her hotel.

Upon arrival, she told Alice that James was in a terrible state. She did not like his drunken behavior around the ranch, but refrained from calling the police, since the papers might hurt his reputation. She also told Alice that James said he was separated from his wife, and that he had lost a lot of money in the market crash. Alice was bewildered, and wondered if they were speaking of the same man. The woman said there was no mistake. She also suggested that it might be best if Alice did not come to the ranch, as she feared more unpleasantness by James if he should see Alice. The proprietress preferred that Alice give her a note for James, and wait to see what would happen.

James came to her hotel room about three hours later, fairly sober but bedraggled. Alice did not question him as to why he had come to Texas, or why he had made those remarks to the ranch woman.

"I think you better go home to your mother," he began. "You can get along without me."

Alice knew he didn't actually want her to go. Usually, after he had sobered from a humiliating drunk, he felt punitive measures necessary against himself. For Alice to leave him seemed to befit his recent actions. They talked for hours. James again suggested that Alice leave him, but she reminded him that they had planned to do his life story together, and that she wouldn't leave until that book was written. She also reminded him that he had promised to dedicate that book to her.

The writing of James' life story had also been suggested by Whitney. Through Alice, he learned about James' boyhood with Bopy and of James foraging on his own when he was about fourteen. The matchless saga of his life seemed a natural for the printed word, and Whitney had on a few occasions urged its writing. It had, he felt, all the marvelous adventure that could top *Smoky*.

James agreed to write his life story. When it was finished, he told her, she was to leave him. She rented two typewriters, as James wasn't too steady for writing legible longhand. Alice wrote to her mother and to Fred explaining what she and James were going to do. She called Whitney also, who immediately became excited about the book's prospects. He instructed Alice to start sending in the chapters as they were finished. Type would be set and chapter proofs returned immediately.

Four months of typing by Alice divulged to her for the first time the complete story of James' life. She venerated him, and excused many of his irritating ways because the life he had led was so different from that of most men. She felt sorry for him, and wondered if a man who had always been so alone, so self-reliant, should ever have married. He had often told her that he couldn't help himself for the way he acted at times. Maybe, Alice thought, he was being truthful: he couldn't help himself.

James interrupted his writing of *Lone Cowboy* to do a review of Charlie Russell's *Good Medicine*, for the *New York Herald Tribune*. The book was a collection of letters by the artist and were assembled by his wife, Nancy. James also wrote an introduction for *French Heels to Spurs*, by Loraine Fielding, a story of an easterner going to a dude ranch in the west.

James and Alice were writing about six hours a day, and in the evenings James worked on the drawings to accompany the story. Maxwell Perkins called constantly, and revealed how excited he was about the book. "It could only happen in the west," he told Alice.

By May 1930, *Lone Cowboy* was finished, and the Jameses returned to Montana. James' bitter thoughts that Alice should leave after the book was finished, seemed to have been forgotten. The only recent argument was when James at first refused to mention in the book that he had married. He thought it detracted from the idea of his being a "Lone Cowboy." Alice insisted that his marriage — denoting the end of his roving days — gave the book a proper and normal ending.

Scribner's, who had for years now, hailed Will James as *the* writer on rodeos, round-ups, ranch life, cowboys, horses, stampedes and the whole west, now gave the public, *Lone Cowboy, My Life Story*, by Will James. Reviews were enthusiastic, and the book scored rapid sales. The *Review of Reviews* stated, "If there is anywhere a cowboy saga, we have it here . . ."[2] The Book-of-the-Month Club made it their August 1930 selection, and there was even some talk that the book might be made into a motion picture. At the year's end, James' autobiography ranked fifth as a best seller in the non-fiction list of 1930[3] and boosted him to the apex of his career. Only he knew, however, that with *Lone Cowboy* his career was balanced on a precarious suppression of his true credentials.

[2]The *Review of Reviews*, October, 1930.
[3]*Sixty Years of Best Sellers*—1895-1955, p. 149.

WILL JAMES

—*Curtis Photos, Los Angeles.*

Chapter Thirteen

LONE COWBOY is the story of a man alone; and nowhere else but in the North American West could such an escapade be possible or such vitality in that way of life come upon one man. To the imagination already bent to the idea of a glorified west, *Lone Cowboy* sharpens and refines, excites and stirs the imagination, but not in sweeping generalities. Instead, it focuses on one man living that adventure — Will James — and crystallizes for a reader's identification with the story.

Some critics of *Lone Cowboy* have expressed that parts of the book are the finest narratives James has written. For a qualifying consideration, one can detect a refreshing perspective to the theme of man in the west. Simply written and nostalgically motivated, *Lone Cowboy* shares the feeling of the *high lonesome* when James rides the mountain country. You cross the creeks, ride the desert country with him and always, you sense the esteem and respect he has for the horse and the land. And although some of the facts are fiction, *Lone Cowboy* still has enough sincerity and tap root animation to be an affirmation of James' love of the cowboy way of life.

But the greatest spectrum of *Lone Cowboy,* the emotional and ambient account of James' early orphanage and adoption by Bopy, the trapper, is a mirage; a lie that began with the lightness of a snowflake in James' mind and turned into an avalanche. The facts are fiction and yet, beyond the margin of the lie itself, there is recognition that the love of the west and the courage of young Will James in *Lone Cowboy* were no less than when he was known as Ernest Dufault who, at the age of fifteen, left his home in eastern Canada to venture as a cowboy in the west. At that time Ernest was not unlike many boys in the east whose dormant spirit of adventure had been stirred and made restless by tales of westerners in pulp magazines. He liked the cowboys, the wide open spaces, but above all — a love for the horse anchored Ernest to a persistent longing to someday go west and become a cowboy.

James was born Joseph-Ernest-Nephtali Dufault on June 6, 1892, at St. Nazaire de Acton, the province of Quebec, and of French parentage. His father, Jean, was a merchant and his mother, Josephine, a deeply religious and devoted mother. Both parents were born in Quebec province: Jean Dufault at St. Nazaire de Acton in 1852, and his wife, thirty-miles away at St. Ours, in 1863. Shortly after James' birth the family moved to Montreal, where James grew up.

Ernest was the second child born. An older brother was named Phillipe, and another, Auguste, was seven years younger than Ernest. Three sisters completed the family: Anna, who later became the Reverend Sister Cajetan, Eugenia, and Helene. Of all the children, Ernest was the most sensitive and intent. He loved to draw, and the use of a pencil or crayon came to him as naturally as life gave him the involuntary act of breathing. By the time he was five, his parents were awed to see Ernest lie on the kitchen floor and on a piece of wrapping paper draw pictures of cats, dogs and horses; not as childish scribblings, but with attention to proportion and detail. Ernest's mother was certain that God had blessed her family with a child genius.

Before he was ten, however, an accident almost took his life. He had come into the kitchen and seeing a bottle of white liquid on the kitchen table, he thought it to be milk, and drank

from it. The bottle held liquid lye. Ernest's screams brought his
mother rushing into the kitchen. She quickly forced him to drink
milk to ease the burning pains and sent Phillipe for the family
doctor. When he arrived, the doctor induced Ernest to vomit.
Later, he told Ernest's mother that her quick action had saved
Ernest. But for a year, he was a sickly boy. It pained him to eat
and while his stomach healed from the burns, he stayed on a
liquid diet.

Ernest's father owned the *Hotel Union,* a small boarding place
where Ernest could collect abandoned pulp magazines with their
action stories and illustrations. He couldn't read or understand
English, but would cut out the illustrations to save and copy.

With his brothers and sisters, Ernest went to a Catholic paro-
chial school. As each of the boys completed his primary school,
he turned to work to help support the family. Ernest worked as
a bellboy and kitchen helper at some of the local hotels, and often
he earned extra money by sketching with soap pictures of horses
and trapping scenes on the plate glass mirrors behind bars of
saloons and hotels.

Trappers were abundant in Canada at the turn of the century
and their gathering spots were favorite haunts for Ernest. There
he heard the trappers tell tales of the white wilderness to the
north, and of the animals that inhabited it. While the trappers
told their stories, Ernest would frequently sketch their descriptions. He became an avid listener of the trappers' stories, and it
is from this association that James wove the story of his life with
Bopy in *Lone Cowboy.*

While trappers and their tales aroused Ernest and sparked his
desire to also travel to country wild and primitive, it was the
love of the horse that became the focal point of all he dreamed
to do in his life.

He often told Auguste he wanted to ride horses in the wide
open spaces which, as Ernest Dufault or Will James, was the

one spell that clearly dominated his entire life. Throughout his formative years, his dreams to go west never faltered. He had often proclaimed to his father that he wanted someday to be a cowboy, but this was accepted as youthful infatuation that would pass.

When he was fifteen he announced to his mother and father that he was going to the Canadian west. They did not want him to leave, but his father seemed to know that with or without permission, Ernest would go. His mother thought him too sensitive to be alone and on his own. Ironically, it was this same sensitivity to a calling that was his courage and drive. In 1907, with ten dollars from his father, and the prayers of his mother, Ernest went west.

The satisfactions that came to him as he traveled westward, seeing the country change from small, congested communities, then through the holy portal of the wide expanses of western Canada, must have been a rare pleasure to those wild longings in his heart. For three years he stayed in the Saskatchewan and Alberta country along the U.S. border. Presumably, some of the jobs were not unlike what *Lone Cowboy* describes, after Bopy has drowned and Billy is on his own. Nighthawking, helping the cook, cutting wood and at every chance working horses and livestock, are all plausible pursuits for a youngster on his own and willing to learn the cowman trade. Even some of the amusing incidents described in *Lone Cowboy* are probably those of Ernest when he learns to smoke and takes his first drink, or when one of the riders sees Billy incessantly scratching himself, tells him, "Why, you little son of a seacook . . . your lousy as a pet coon."

Ernest's first visit home was in 1910. He stayed only briefly, and returned to Alberta. It was probably just before Ernest went home that he had his first encounter with the law. It has been mentioned that when James was enrolled at Yale he did some loose talking, through liquor, that he had once been on death row in Canada and had escaped by burning a log cabin jail. Again, while intoxicated (in the early thirties) he made the same remark to Alice, and she let it pass without giving it much significance. In *Lone Cowboy*, James relates an incident involving a sheepherder in a bar, a fracas that has James confined in a post stockade of the Royal Canadian Mounted Police.[1] A sheepherder became indignant, — "on the prod" — and pulled a razor and cut across James' left ear and down his cheek. James shot the herder. In a dazed state, and after receiving medical treatment, James returned to his hotel room. Shortly after, the Mounted Police came and arrested him. The next morning, James was told that the sheepherder had died. For weeks James was confined and then suddenly was released. He went back to the bar where the trouble had happened to see the bartender who was there the evening James shot the herder. James was informed that the bartender was no longer working, because he was in jail for shooting a sheepman. As it happened, the herder ran out of the bar when James shot him. After James returned to his room, the herder returned to the bar and began to pick on the bartender, who promptly obliged the "scrap" by spinning him with another bullet. The bartender, believing he had killed the man, ran away, and James was held. The herder was near death for some time, and not until after the police were able to gather the complete story did they release James.

James probably reworked the facts about the sheepherder incident when he wrote the story in *Lone Cowboy*, as he also doctored the facts about the cattle rustling in eastern Nevada. Whether the herder died or not is unknown. But if James did burn the jail and escape, as he said while intoxicated, it may have been after the escape that he went home in 1910, for im-

[1]The author has no success verifying these facts. Royal Canadian Police records of this time were vague and often ephemeral. Still, what facts there are fit together.

mediately after he returned to western Canada he advised his family to address their letters to him as C. W. Jackson and that he was going to cross the border into Montana. Dropping his French-Canadian name and going to Montana, he said, would offer better opportunities for himself. A few months later he changed his name again and told his family to address him as W. R. James, and later, as Will James.

About the summer of 1910, James crossed back into Saskatchewan. At Gull Lake, in the southwest corner of that Canadian province, he asked for a job from Fred Jackson, who was running the round-up wagons for the 76 Cattle Company. Jackson was then in his early twenties, and remembers James riding a "fuzz tail of a horse who couldn't throw a wet saddle blanket." James wanted to hire on as a buckaroo. "Somehow," says Jackson, "he just didn't look like a buckaroo. He was awkward looking on a horse. I offered him a job as wrangler, and he took it. He was an awful poor cowboy at the time, and no good in my book."

Jackson took a dislike to James, because James couldn't measure up to his boasts of being a top hand. James wrangled for two months — left a flock of drawings for some of the riders — and quit at the company headquarters at Crane Lake, up north on the Canadian National Railroad.

Ed Blackmore, a *ranny* of the Rocky Mountain country, provides what is at this time, the earliest account of Will James after he came into the United States.[2] James was about eighteen when Blackmore met him . . .

"The summer of 1911, I planned to go to the Big Piney country of Wyoming. I heard they paid good wages for hay hands here. I wanted a little stake for the winter months ahead. I was at Orchard, Colorado, at the time, about 40 miles east of Greeley on the South Platte River. I had two good saddle horses and a good outfit, about everything a

[2]This account was first published in the *Denver Westerner's Brand Book,* 1962, as part of an article on Will James, by Bob Cormack.

'ranny hand' would use. I put my bed and grub on one horse and rode the other, and headed out for Big Piney.

"I was in no hurry, and in about two weeks I landed a job at a big hay-camp close to Big Piney. I stayed there about fifteen days. The Mosquitoes and deer flies were so bad that I decided I didn't like the country, so I decided to move on west to Vail, Oregon. My horses were in good shape, so I went across country to American Falls, Idaho. I crossed the Snake River there and went on west to Rupert, Idaho. I stopped there to get some grub and smoking tobacco, and decided to stay all night. I put my horses in a livery stable and my bed in an empty stall.

"I then went uptown and stopped at a pool hall. It was about 7 p.m. I got to talking to a man who looked like a stockman. I wanted to know how times were around there and how work was. I learned he was John Hagberry, who had a horse-camp south of there. He said he could use another man, and offered me a job helping trap wild horses. I thought I would give it a try.

"The next morning we left town about 6:30. We headed south, crossed the Snake River and traveled until about noon. John had a four-up on a good wagon and a pretty good load: grub, rope, wire and other supplies. He stopped at a creek and watered and fed the horses. He said it was about 45 or 50 miles from Rupert to camp. We pulled into camp about seven that evening.

"John's two brothers, Lew[3] and Ronald, and a fella named Bill James were at camp. I was told who they were and I told them who I was. They had just finished building a new horse trap, and were ready to start chasing horses. In a few days we got started.

"There were five of us working together. After I had been there a couple of weeks and had been a good hand, willing to work hard, they got pretty friendly with me. I liked Bill because he seemed to do things the easy way. He was older than I was, so I did as he told me to. Bill and I rode together quite a lot and got acquainted a little.

[3]Quite definitely the Lew Hackberry James rustled cattle with in eastern Nevada.

"Around camp, I noticed Bill drawing pictures of horses and women, and cowmen and animals. I picked up some of the drawings I liked and saved them. When we moved camp, I gathered up some more of them. Some were very good and some I thought were poor. I kept the sketches in my bed, next to the tarpaulin. I mailed a few drawings to my mother to keep for me.

"Along about the first of October, we quit chasing horses and started to gather all the ones we already caught. About the middle of November, Bill went to Montana for Thanksgiving and Christmas. I left my horses at the camp and went to Cheyenne, on the train. We were to come back by the first of February, 1912. It was a hard winter, lots of snow and cold as the North Pole.

"When I got back to camp about February first, the Hagberry boys had moved the horses close to Snake River and were feeding them hay. Bill James came back about the first of March, 1912. Along in April, they shipped 400 head of horses to Miles City, Montana. Then we went back to chasing horses again. Near the middle of August, they quit chasing. Bill and I got our horses together and decided to trail them to Miles City and sell them. There was a good horse-market there then.

"Bill had five head of broke horses and I traded my two broke horses for ten head of unbroke horses to a cow outfit. I had another five head from the Hagberry boys — altogether fifteen head. Bill and I gathered another eighteen head, so we had thirty-three horses to trail for about five hundred miles. This is when I really got acquainted with Bill James.

"We were about a month going to Montana, back past the Big Piney country, north of Three Forks, over the head of Powder River, and north and east to Miles City, trailing right down Powder River. We sold our horses, and had a good time for about a week. I sacked my saddle, rolled up my bed and caught a train for Cheyenne. Bill went on to Billings."

Will James was a wanderer; a weed in a great garden, never fixed to one place or environment, but apparently popping up wherever a wind or a whim had drifted him. In those early years in the saddle he sauntered between Canada and Montana, then into Idaho and eventually drifting south. Some of the hearsay stories about him in Montana indicate that he was not esteemed as a rider and bronc-buster. Probably this is accurate information since James lacked experience. It could also account for his roaming through Montana, Wyoming, Idaho, California, and Nevada; to learn and then go on to new territory where he would be accepted with better measure as a rider. But he also drifted because he loved seeing new country. If there is an essence of a spirit of Will James, it is this lone cowboy aura in a classical land of space and silence and close to nature . . . "on top of a good feeling pony, the morning sun shining on fresh green sod, trees a budding and millions of birds a singing everywhere . . ." and with no room in his chest for anything excepting . . . "what was all around, under, above, and ahead of me . . ."

In this free, drifting world of his he learned of country critters and of range history from the golden memories of old timers, and some of them became his own imagined heritage.

When his first book, *Cowboys North and South,* was announced in the Reno *Evening Gazette,* the editor's request for a short biographical article brought this fanciful note from James:[4]

"My folks before me was range folks, my granddad's grandaddy made his own saddles, braided his own ropes, and worked the rawhide for his own chaps, there was no saddle shops then, cattle wasn't even branded, no shipping was done and a critter's hide was worth more than the beef she was packing underneath.

"My folks seen them times and on till when the first railroad come west; it's right about then that branding irons was recorded quick, rustlers was hung and the cattle game growed till the longhorns lost their speed and gradually the white faced Hereford took hold, now they're in to stay the

[4]*Reno Evening Gazette,* October 26, 1924.

same as the cowboy which lots of people are wanting to put on the list of history and past.

"I'm a descendant of the folks that's seen the cattle game from the start on till today, them generations before me leaves me the same as them, there's nothing but range blood in my veins and that's why I say that even tho I did turn to writing and drawing I'm still all cowboy. I might wear a cap and Douglas shoes at times, I've even drank tea and talked over radio, but I still roll my own and what I call my home is where I can hear the critters bellern, broncs a pawing the earth by my door and good old cow ponies a waiting for the feel of the rein."

Greater embroidery of his inspired heritage rests with the ambient and poignant Bopy, and he might have been invented by James to excuse his French accent. James spoke only French while in eastern Canada, although a smattering of broken English may have been part of his knowledge. In any case, it was in western Canada that he learned English. But throughout all his life he carried in his voice French intonations. To excuse this accent and its betrayal that James was not western born on the sod of the Judith Gap in Montana, he may have then invented the story of Bopy. To James, a cover-up was imperative because he felt that unless a man were born in the west he could never be capable of becoming a top hand. Bopy was convenient and plausible. It even surpassed all the beauty, as James visioned, of being born in the west. More than anything the story gave him a claim to a heritage that was far above the legacy of one western born. It directed attention to him which he relished; made him the core that effected awe and reverence from his friends. Thus, by the time James had settled for Nevada as the range country to work, he was considered a top hand, and behind that experience was a life that had sprung from the western soil as strong and as natural as sagebrush.

James went home to Canada only three times in his life after his first departure: 1910, 1925, and in 1934.

By 1925, he was married, and developing into a popular raconteur of the west. He told Alice about the middle of that year that he would have to travel to New York to see *Scribner's* on business and since he could not afford the expense for both of them to go, Alice would have to stay in Nevada.

James did not indicate when he might return. But Alice eventually became aware that his stay seemed excessive, and she called Whitney Darrow, who told her that Bill had left New York over a week before. She did not, of course, have any knowledge that he had a home in Canada. When James did return to Nevada he excused his lateness by saying he had visited with friends in Montana. Alice became annoyed, as he had told her he did not have enough money to take her to New York with him, but had obviously spent extra money they could not afford. She was upset, too, because he had not written her.

Over the years, from 1907 to 1934, the Dufault family had accumulated many letters, telegrams, pictures and drawings that James had sent to them. James knew that his mother worried about him, and while many of his letters and messages to her were brief, they at least indicated he was well and happy. After the death of his father in 1926, James wrote only to his brother Auguste. He expressed concern about the health of his mother, who had been failing, and who was now living with Auguste and his family. James instructed Auguste to do all that he could for their mother, to buy her a present from time to time, and to say it had come from Ernest. James promised Auguste that someday when his business affairs were in better order, he would make adjustments to Auguste for assuming his (James') responsibility to their mother. In a later letter, James told Auguste that he was developing a ranch, and their mother, Auguste, and his family, should soon be able to come to Montana and join him.

For years all that James told about himself to Auguste was that he had business interests with a publishing company, but nothing about being a writer. Doubtless, James feared that his family would find this fact too tempting for them to keep a family secret. And secrecy was especially important since he had already concocted the Bopy story.

James' last visit to his Canadian family, in 1934, turned almost immediately into one of revulsion and severe pain for his mother. At this time Will James and *Lone Cowboy* were nationally known. Even Europe enthusiastically received the writings of Will James. The Prince of Denmark was a particular fan, and wrote James to express his delight with *Smoky* and *Lone Cowboy*, and hoped some day to shake the hand of this famous westerner.

With this acclaim and popularity, James became terrified that his true identity would become known. And too, there was the fright of conceivable scandal in Canada and in Montana. James now demanded from Auguste and their mother all correspondence, pictures, drawings, anything that might link Will James to Ernest Dufault, and insisted they be destroyed.

His mother argued and pleaded with James not to destroy the mementoes of her Ernest. But James would not — could not — compromise. Finally all correspondence and art were brought to him, which he promptly burned. At the last moment, he allowed his mother to keep a studio picture of himself, but refused to write any message or signature on the picture. He instructed Auguste to keep it hidden.

Until the time of his father's death in 1926, James wrote to his family in French. Afterwards, he wrote to Auguste and only in English. Their mother could not read or speak English and James instructed Auguste what to tell and not to tell her. James' letters, if handwritten, were signed with the initial *E*, and his typed letters spelled out his name, *Ernest*. Each letter instructed

Auguste to destroy it after having been read, as it would be "a catastrophe if his true identity were known." Sometime in the early thirties James told Auguste with the strictest confidence his Will James pseudonym.

James consistently promised that someday he would have their mother, Auguste and his family move to his Montana ranch. After *Lone Cowboy* had appeared with its wide acceptance, it was beyond hope that James could ever keep that promise if, that is, he ever had had those intentions.

Regardless of *Lone Cowboy*, it would have been complicated enough for James to suddenly spring a different name, parents, sisters, brothers and another life onto Alice and her family, Fred and Dolly and other friends.

During the years following 1930, and particularly 1934, James deteriorated appreciably. Why? No one seems to know or completely understand. Some would say it was success and drinking that were ruining James. Others would blame Alice, because she didn't try to understand him. But underneath all of this was the guilt motivation of *Lone Cowboy*.

James' biography had brought his career to a pinnacle of notoriety and adulation from his public. With crowds and their attentions he was gay, witty and very much in character as the cowboy artist and writer the public expected from him. While from the outside James was riding the crest of the wave, within himself he was drowning, and he could not call or even beg for help. He had a fear of exposure and scandal, and a tormenting guilt which permeated his self-respect. Whenever he was alone with time to think, this fear and guilt shrank his character, and he drank excessively.

Lone Cowboy was both a paradise and a hell for Will James.

To Ed Springer

I'd always give you a fresh horse
if yours was leg weary —
And your cattle, if they drifted
and was in need of feed, I'd
turn them too in my best stack of hay.

Sincerely
WILL JAMES.

FLY LEAF SKETCH
Fly leaf of book James sent to Ed Springer, one of Will James'
benefactors in New Mexico.

— *Courtesy of Ed Springer.*

Chapter Fourteen

WHEN the Jameses arrived home from Texas, Billings was there to greet them. James was by now the popular interpreter and illustrator of the American cowboy. The amount of clamoring for James to speak to local and civic clubs, out-of-state rodeos, and historical societies was prodigious, and he accepted only a few local engagements. His intention was to stay close to the home ranch. Through the local newspaper he expressed urgency in preparing articles and another book for his publishers. Moreover, he didn't want any visitors at his ranch for the summer regardless of who they were — celebrities or otherwise. His home, he told reporters, was his workshop, and the only real relaxation he got was while working. James also wanted peace and quiet to give support to regaining harmony in his and Alice's life.

Also by staying close to the ranch he had more time to be with Fred and Dolly and their son, whom James was allowed to name. He chose Clint, a name that had been a favorite with James and which was undoubtedly what he called himself when his parents addressed their letters to him as C. W. Jackson. Clint was nearly a year old when James returned from Texas, and the "little fella," as James called him, was an immense joy for him.

Alice had often felt that James' refusal to have children stemmed from a dislike of them. It was an erroneous assumption, as Clint in his five years at the ranch would prove. While Clint was the favorite of James, his other nieces and nephews were remembered with books and gifts from their "Uncle Bill." And in New York James' best lectures were given to children who eagerly listened to the famous cowboy.

In retrospect, it is conjectured that James was never able to have children of his own, although he never admitted this to Alice. To Clint, however, James gave all the attentions of a father. He bought western clothes for Clint, and often would take him for walks in the pasture to see the pet deer, or the livestock. A horse called Big Enough was purchased for Clint. After James was finally able to show Clint how to hold onto the saddlehorn, James would mount his horse and, leading Big Enough, go for a ride. Although Fred and Dolly rarely went into town, James encouraged them to take a day or weekend away from the ranch while he and Alice would care for the boy.

Alice's mother and father came to live in Billings in 1930. Fred, and his brother Paul, together with James, made arrangements to establish the father in a small carpentry shop business.

For one year at least, especially that summer and fall, there were happy times at the Rocking R. James had not ceased drinking, but it was accepted that he would now and then be "taking a holiday," as was the family's way of excusing James' absence. The family gathered together on Sundays. Dolly, Alice, her mother and the cook prepared Sunday dinner while James, Fred and his father would go horseback riding, or sit about and talk. Often guests from Billings were invited, usually the Earl Snook family, who had an art supply house in Billings where James bought most of his art needs.

One of the closest personal relationships that endured was between Alice's mother and James. She had considerable influence over him, and loved him no less than her own sons. James was no less affectionate to her and always purchased gifts for her whether he was shopping in Billings, New York or Hollywood. Whenever he presented gifts in person, she would kiss him on the cheek and James would hug her and often say, "You're the only mother I've ever had. Got to keep ya happy."

Mrs. Conradt frequently sided with James in his arguments with Alice. She would tell Alice that she must try to understand him and, above all, must never leave him.

When Alice and her mother had their talks about James, Alice would insist that unless James could be seen when he was at his worst, it was difficult to really understand how he changed. It was an academic question for some years between Alice and her mother, but the test of Alice's proposition did come a few years later, in Hollywood.

Alice's father had also warmed to James, and although he always sensed that there was something about James that didn't ring clearly, he never could pinpoint the suspicions he held.

By 1930 the ranch was in productive order, and Fred had displayed the managerial sense that James had always credited him with. Winters were severe in Montana, but Fred and Dolly never faltered in caring for James' interest while he was in New York or Hollywood for the winter. During the initial development of the ranch, Fred had waived the delinquency of his own salary when almost every penny James was earning was needed for the ranch. The usual employer-employee relationship never did exist between James and Fred. It was much closer, and had roots dating back to their cowboying days in Nevada. Fred did much more than was ever to be expected of a ranch manager. James was not ungrateful and with Clint meaning much to him, James told Fred and Dolly that the boy would have all the education he wanted, and James would foot the bill.

Wisely, James never attempted to interfere in the operations of the ranch. He did have certain ideas, mostly old-fashioned, which Fred had not countered in spite of the expenses involved. But in all aspects of making the ranch pay for itself, James allowed Fred a free choice of decision. Whereas James found comfort in some of the old ways, Fred became excited with the newer developments in ranching and cattle husbandry. He talked over with James what he wanted to do or to try in newer procedures, and James told him to go ahead as he wished. Fred started crossbreeding their Herefords with a Scottish Highlander bull that was a gift to James by a Billings rancher. Fred wanted to produce an animal more capable of withstanding long hard winters on the northern plains. He tried the newer grass varieties in experimental pasture areas. James took an interest in Fred's husbandry and horticulture ventures, but at best it was a token effort. Writing and drawing were his first obligations, and by voice, or in letters, he consistently told Fred to "take care of the ranch, old boy, and I'll try my darndest to bring home the bacon."

James and Alice stayed in Hollywood during the winter of 1930-31. James wrote feverishly and displayed again the enthusiasm that characterized his early writing days. He had completed at the ranch, original sketches on the fly leaves for 250 special copies of *Lone Cowboy*, and following this, started the paintings for the Scribner Illustrated Classics edition of *Lone Cowboy*. The writing and illustrating of his latest book, *Big Enough*, were also accomplished that season in Hollywood.

Chapter Fifteen

BIG ENOUGH appeared serially in *Blue Book Magazine* in the fall of 1931, and was released concurrently in book form. Another anthology of James short stories, consisting of selections taken from *Cowboys North and South* and *Drifting Cowboy*, came out that same year, and was entitled: *Sun Up; Tales of the Cow Camps*. Whitney Darrow had selected the stories as a special book for the Junior Literary Guild.

Big Enough is the story of a cowboy and a cowhorse born on the same day and "... growed up together to where they were big enough — Big Enough for most anything." James dedicated the book to Clint.

James envisioned *Big Enough* as another *Smoky*, and *The Saturday Review of Literature* was of the opinion that James' latest book was one of the few really great horse stories in the English language.[1] Actually, *Big Enough* is not that good, nor does it have the originality and perennial appeal of *Smoky*. The book opens with interest and feeling and then tends to drift to a rambling narrative and a style that becomes more difficult to follow.

Big Enough is nonetheless a pleasant story to read. But if one follows a critical approach by rating the story in comparison to the best work of an author, *Big Enough* lacks the verity and mar-

[1]*Saturday Review of Literature*, December 5, 1931.

velous empathy that is the hallmark of *Smoky* or *Lone Cowboy*.
When James allows human characters to consistently predomi-
nate his narrative, they differ slightly from thousands of other
fictional characterizations who spoke their lines without being
immortalized and were forgotten — and with them, the entire
book. *Lone Cowboy* is an exception, and enhances the rendition
of words because James wrote with a very personal and moving
emotion. It was an affirmation of love. His other novels lack personal truth. *Sand* is an example of this lameness when James has
to use myths of the west and his personal prejudices as a crutch
for his fictional tales. In particular, James amused his readers
with shy cowboy episodes of the western fairy tale.

"... and when she grabbed me by the arm and pulled
me down right close by her I knew my heart lost many a
beat ..."

Ross Santee, who frequently reviewed James' books, has noted
that... "James can get sentimental about a horse and it never
bothers me, but when he writes about a girl, I always skip that
piece. Anytime he gets away from the things he has lived and
seen, and drags a woman into his pieces, they are apt to get
pretty thin. But when James writes about the open range, I can
always smell the sage."

Certainly James was far from the shy, unassuming cowboy that
some of his stories describe. Anyone who worked the cow country
as long as James stopped blushing many campfire talks ago with
other cowboys. But James played upon one of the sentiments his
eastern audiences enjoyed reading about. Maybe James didn't
relish writing these exaggerations — he had expressed distaste to
those passages — but he was also told that to sell books he had
to give the public what it wanted.

Another finger-poking slant by James was with dudes; awkward
characters asking the silliest questions and doing damn foolish
actions around livestock. James actually detested those dudes

who came west with *high-fallutin'* attitudes about themselves and their *more civilized* home back east. James never hesitated to describe them with reference to the back profile of a donkey. In his *Home Ranch* James has an eastern family annoying the hell out of an outfit which is trying to work their cattle on the open range. The daughter, "a pretty fair looking young lady . . ." is anxious to walk out into the range and see the nice cows. The round-up cook, hearing that, sets forth this bit of advice:

"I sure wouldn't get in sight of the herd if I was you folks," he says . . .

"What would they do?" asks the daughter, disappointed.

"They'd do enough to make you wish there was a tree close to climb up on."

"You mean they'd charge a person?"

"Yes, and catch up with it quick and scatter the carcass till there'd be no remains to be found," says the cook, half peeved at such ignorant questions . . .

At another time, the father of the young lady is wondering to the cook why the cowboys don't do any fishing. The cook tells him that there isn't much time for that. The dude answers, ". . . not much sport going on around here then, eh?"

The cook looked up from the batter he was mixing. "I don't know just what you call sport," he says, "but I think if you'd drop your rope on a mad cow while you're riding a spooky bronc, that you'd find plenty of excitement, and need a heap more skill in playing your line so's it won't get around you and cut you in two, than any skill needed to land a poor fish . . ."

James' motives are distinct in his story telling about dudes. They are silly in the outstart, but in the end it is the cowboy, patient and silently grinning at these *gazabos* that sets the dude straight on how a man acts in the west.

Occasionally James employed the gun to move the action of his stories, although he abhorred its excessive use in western novels. He believed that the western story had been plagued with quick-triggered guns, and consequently gave a gross misinterpretation of the west.

"For those run-of-the-mill smoke and thunder sort of western novels," James said, "there is everything in it that will please them that don't know the west . . .

"I don't object to guns, as long as they aint pointed towards me, what I object at, by making that big fuss over 'em, is that so much that's good in the western life is covered up by 'em."[2]

James' contempt for these stories was no less than for the synthetic manufacturers who wrote them. B. M. Bower (Bertha Sinclair) was one of the few western writers James respected. "Bower," commented James, "is one of the mighty few western writers who can write a book, have a few shooting scrapes in it, and still have plenty of room to show a cowboy at work."[3]

James read infrequently, and only themes telling about real cowboys at work preserved his patience. Even then he could be critical of a writer's approach to that theme and find picayune faults with the interpretation of facts. But, James in his way, was as guilty. He tended to be overly-sentimental and ascribed to the cowboy the vestiges of true manhood, independence and self-reliance.

Still, James' cowboys do not emerge as virtuous heroes *a la* the cinema cowboy or the western novel. He shook his pen and brought out the cowboy as a horseman, livestock man or a drifter, who basically was lazy to any chore that took him off his horse, and who could easily get himself into some sort of trouble. The ultra-good or the ultra-bad cowboy as the movies and novels displayed were extremes, and for James were not worthy of attention.

James prided himself on his fidelity in writing about the cow-

[2]"Far West and Near West," in *Bookman,* August, 1928.
[3]*Ibid.*

boy. And while his writing became repetitious and somewhat dramatized as he went on, he did show the manner of speaking, the casual daily life and livestock-centered interests of the working cowboy. He knew too, that by showing the cowboy as he really was, he also debunked the western writers who hunt material, "by going through the country on a Pullman, afraid to mix in the dust and get the facts."

Predominantly in James' mind were Zane Grey and Clarence Mulford who were the popular contemporaries whose novels were built around guns and *good guys* and *bad guys.*

But to lionize James as the apostle of sensible writing about the cowboy and the west in a natural and unpedantic way is fallacious. Another, Ross Santee, occupies a high step in the naturalistic school of cowboy writing. Moreover, Santee is measured above James by some who dwell on comparative studies of range and cowboy literature. In any case, Will James was the favorite with the public, and especially in the east. His books had the warm effect of being a welcomed letter from a friend, enhanced by James placing a small drawing, after his introduction, of himself on a horse and holding the reins of another horse and saying, "Here's a gentle horse for you — climb on and follow me." As long as the public welcomed what he wrote, James was immune to what critics wished to spout about his books. The one exception, already mentioned, was criticism of his language and his grammar. He was proud of his cowboy vernacular.

Thus, in *Cowboys North and South,* James says in his preface:

> "What I've wrote in this book is without the help of the dictionary or any course in story writing. I didn't want to dilute what I had to say with a lot of imported words that I couldn't of handled. Good english is all right, but when I want to say *something* I believe in hitting straight to the point without fishing for decorated language...
>
> "... but as the editors and publishers seem to like my efforts the way I put 'em out, which is natural and undiluted

... makes me feel confident enough to give my pen full swing without picking up the slack."

Literary critics complimented James' first works as interesting in light of the language and the unusual hum of words and grammar which, if not academic, were at least an honesty from the range land. For some critics, year in and year out reviewing of James books became tiresome and impatient reading. One reviewer of James' *Three Mustangeers* stated: "Although not troublesome in *Smoky* and *Lone Cowboy*, Mr. James' ungrammatical style is becoming a bit weary. His latest book would be just as readable and fully as entertaining if a few of the more rudimentary rules of grammar were observed."[4]

It is doubtful that James' bad grammar was the reason for annoyance. Actually, it was because his stories were shallow and lacked stimulation, and the bad grammar sorely stood out. Novelty is only boredom when the novelty lacks conviction. *Smoky* and *Lone Cowboy* are James' supreme examples of conviction, and of the language subtly blending with the stories.

Frank Scully, reflecting in his book, *Armour Bright*,[5] about his acquaintance with authors, says of James and others who write as he did: "These men with no formal education, learn to use language, not to be used by it ..."

James probably could not have recognized a noun from a verb, but his choice of action verbs bears truth to Scully's clever observation. James could use language. Slang, colloquialisms, similes and range jargon were easy for him, and he used this speech with vivid and forceful denotation. In describing the various sorts of bucking horses, James says:

"And again there's the horse that keeps his brain a-working for some way to hang his rider's hide on the corral or anywhere it'll hang, and save his own hide doing it. He's crooked anyway you take him, and will put so much energy in his bucking that when he's up in the air all twisted up, he don't figure or care about the coming down. He'll make his cowboy shake hands with Saint Peter, and won't worry whether the ground is under or on the side of him when he hits. When he falls, he falls hard, and the rider has little chance to get away. The pony seldom gets hurt, he's wise enough to look out for himself; what's on top of him is what he wants to get rid of, and he won't be on the square trying it . . ."[6]

And when Smoky, the one-man horse, is mounted with the "feel of a strange hand," Smoky rids himself of his rider easily. Then: "A few riders rushed up to find the cowboy setting up and shaking his head like trying to get back amongst the living . . ."

Many authors have tried to describe the human mental upset when hit on the head. James' concise expression, without detailed description of whirling dizziness and what have you, strikes perfectly with . . . "trying to get back amongst the living . . ."

In a less vibrant mood, but still tightly descriptive, James in the opening pages of *Smoky* describes the foal's first hours after birth:

"His mammy was close by him, and at the first move the colt made she run her nose along his short neck and nickered. Smoky's head went up another two inches at the sound, and his first little answering nicker was heard. Of course a person would have had to listen mighty close to hear it, but then if you'd a watched his nostrils quivering you could tell that's just what he was trying to do . . ."

James wrote his stories no differently than the way he told them aloud. His written thoughts divide themselves into sentences by context and natural pause, not by rules of grammar. He lets his pen breathe and pause naturally to determine the punctuation.

[6]"Bucking Horses and Bucking Horse Riders," in *Cowboys North and South.*

James' writing, unless one wishes to be puritanical about it all, is actually a highly developed mode of expression. Again, speaking of his best works, they are vivid and sincere; salty in understatement, satire and hyperbole. Charles Twichell, son of Burton Twichell, recalls that a certain professor of English at Yale told James that he could write better than any pedant.

But if the purist is inclined to dissect James' English, he will find much to amuse himself; e.g., the word education spelled ... *edducation, edication, eddication* and *education*. Creature, James spells ... *crethure* and *creathure*. Often on the same page a word is spelled at least two different ways.

Whatever the grammatical rule, James has most likely given it a twist. A rule determines a path, and the more rules, the narrower the path. James, unhindered by most writing rules, expressed himself without inhibitions.

James was also a poet.

On some tattered drawings, signed 1914 and 1915, and in the possession of Mrs. James Riordan,[7] James sketched a gentleman attired in a tuxedo looking aghast at a man hanging from a tree. The verse reads:

A Man i know searched far an' wide a tryin' for to see
What sort of folks had roosted highest in his family tree.
He started in to climbin', but come shinnin' down with vim
With visions of his grandad a hangin' from a lim'.

Again, on the lighter side of his poetic dabbling, James relates his feelings about Hollywood when he was an extra in western movies.

[7]At the time the Riordans were ranch owners in eastern Nevada.

BACK TO THE RANGE

I've played the moving picture game
    And worked it good and hard
But it's too all fired tame
    For real cowpunchers, pard.
Them actor guys are tenderfeet
    That never saw the range,
And when they hit the saddle seat
    Their ridin's fierce an' strange.

They put us through a lot o' stunts
    That punchers never do
A fellow feels just like a dunce
    Before he gets half through
It's all a lot of honey-mush
    About some gal, you see
Twould make an honest puncher blush
    Sich goin's on to see.

Because out on the range, you know,
    Around the chaparral
We never had no time to go
    Close-herdin' any gal.
They's too much rustlin' round for strays
    Or else a breakin' broncs
Or branding calves on roundup days
    For any such nonsense.

They ain't a cuss in all the bunch
    Kin cinch up a saddle right
T'would fetch a snort from a cowpunch
    Their togs is just a fright.
The other day I was most floored
    Whilst watching of the boss
For in a film he climbed aboard
    The Injun side of his haws.

I'm sick of all sich sights as those
    I'm quitting an' goin' back there
Among a regular bunch that knows
    Range ridin' for fair.
I'll strike for my old stompin' ground
    Where range life is lived true
Where there's no greener around
    To tell me what to do.[8]

[8]In the possession of Mrs. Eleanor Snook, Billings, Montana.

Chapter Sixteen

THE WHIRLWIND stirred by James since being accepted as the popular interpreter of the cowboy in the west had created a great vortex. It had drawn to him all the good and bad things of life that James had said, "all come at once."

By spring of 1933, there had been enough happenings to run the gamut of his emotions. *Big Enough* and *Sun Up* sold well, and *Lone Cowboy*, in its classical edition with seven color plates, was on par with *Smoky* in popular appeal.

That same year one of his better novels, *Three Mustangeers*, was released and issued the year before was the *Drifting Cowboy Series*, a five volume set consisting of *Big Enough, Lone Cowboy, Sand, Smoky*, and *Sun Up*.

His status as a lecturer at some of the art schools had by now bolstered his reputation as an artist.

Isabelle Johnson, a Billings artist, remembers when James visited the Otis Institute at Los Angeles, in 1930, while she was a student:

> "I was as surprised, as were the other students, at his knowledge of the structure of the horse. He made complete sketches of the horse in action; the colt in relation to the horse, the bony structure of the knee, its muscular structure and using anatomically correct terminology in each instance. His shy manner and quiet voice were in direct contrast to the positive lines flowing from his drawing arm and turning every joint and muscle of his subject into life."

James' subtle humor, effective storytelling and art demonstrations were enticements for his appearance at lecture halls and autograph parties. While some lecture committees turned cool when it was suggested that a *cowboy* appear before their audience, invariably they were pleased with James' presentations. One might, however, have to be prepared for some lack of conventions by James. George Snell, of Billings, had invited James to give a talk at a Kiwanis meeting. With a sense of precaution, Snell asked James not to do any drinking until after the talk. "Don't worry, George," assured James. "But I do worry," Snell emphasized.

James arrived sober at the meeting, just as it was being called to order. Instead of seating himself in the place reserved for him next to Snell, James sat on the opposite side of the long dinner table, with his back to the rest of the members. When introduced, James calmly stood on his chair and then onto the table, turned and delivered his talk.

"We were taken aback by James' behavior," says Snell, "but within minutes, with his dry humor and easy way of talking, he had won the club members' esteem and appreciation. You couldn't help liking the man."

By far James' greatest thrill was in the winter of 1932, when Paramount Studios purchased the movie rights to *Lone Cowboy*. And, while in Hollywood later that summer, advising on the scenario of *Lone Cowboy*, James was informed that Fox Studios had purchased *Smoky*.

These were the good things.

The bad things began with the death of Alice's father in July of 1932, about a year after he and his wife moved to Billings.

His death shattered one of the more pleasant years on the James ranch. James himself admitted that those times were a fulfillment in having a mother and father to care about. James insisted on paying all of the funeral expenses, and that Alice's father have a new suit for burial. After the funeral, Alice accompanied her mother back to Reno, where Alice stayed for a few weeks before returning to Billings. In her absence, James began the devastating habit of drinking while he wrote. His past addiction to alcohol, although excessive, was at least confined to outside his studio. Why he began to drink during his working schedule is indistinct. Remorse over the death of Alice's father — or silent guilts about his own family in Canada — or the combination of both — might have started the calamitous turn. And possibly his studio drinking was an expedient to speed up his writing since he was behind schedule. Whatever the reason, it was the beginning of a rapid end for James. He was to be no exception to the fate of any writer who must drink to produce.

In the summer of 1933, James was in Hollywood in conjunction with his autobiography adaptation to the screen. Alice arrived in Hollywood later when James received a $10,000 check for the *Smoky* movie rights.

Hollywood's way of life, with the extreme publicity given him by the studios, was a natural for his one weakness. He surrendered easily to Hollywood's social whirl, and its attraction for James infuriated Alice. She was constantly embarrassed by his actions, and studio officials at Fox became apprehensive of his drinking since James was scheduled to narrate *Smoky.*

Hoping to discourage his drinking, Alice invited her mother to Hollywood on the pretense of watching some of the studio shots of *Smoky* being filmed. For a few days, James stayed sober while Mother was present. On the fourth evening, he failed to return from the studio.

The next night some polo players from Santa Barbara brought James home virtually unconscious from drinking. Alice was beside herself, and with the help of one of the polo players, Alice's mother put James to bed. He insisted that his "liquor jug" be put on the night table. Mother promised that she would, but emptied the bottle that was in James' hip pocket and filled it with tea. She locked the bedroom door, and sat in a chair the entire night outside James' bedroom. In the early morning, James went into a tantrum and cussed Alice and her mother for the tea in his jug. The next day Alice pin-pointed her frustrations about James to her mother, as she had tried to do for some years. Now Mother had seen James at his worst, but still she would not let Alice run James down. "He's a good man," she told Alice. "We've got to find a way to bring Bill out of this."

Later that day Alice confronted James with his actions, and the obscene language he had used, and about Mother sitting all night outside his door. It rocked James to utter disgust of himself, and he cried. He swore he would never drink again, and apologized profusely to Mother. A day later Mother returned to Reno with a promise from James that he would behave, and to stop "worrying those nice men from the studios."

Most of the *Smoky* film had been shot around Flagstaff, Arizona. In preliminary discussions with the producers, James suggested filming at the ranch of his benefactor, Ed Springer in New Mexico. But Fox finally settled their cameras on the red rock country of Northern Arizona.

The most impressive member of the *Smoky* cast, at least to James, was the horse that played the part of his famous equine. The horse's name was Rex, a veteran star of the silent days when he was billed as *King of the Wild Horses*. James at first did not care for a black stallion playing the part since his story clearly said that Smoky was *mouse color*. James visited the Jones Stable, where years before he worked as a stuntman and rider for silent westerns, to watch a demonstration of why Rex, black or otherwise, was ideal for the picture. Rex was camera wise. His years of movie making had proven him to be a reliable performer, wise to cues, and dependable while working without restraints in front of the cameras. Consequently, the studio did not have to go to additional expense to train another horse just to satisfy a color requirement.

From director Eugene Forde's point of view, Rex was a natural because of his "tremendous personality." Rex was dangerous, however, and at times vicious. He would fight with little provocation, and this was what Forde wanted for the scenes where Smoky fights that *feeling of a strange hand*.

The horse, by the way, did fight all too convincingly. During the filming of the scene where Smoky fights two cowboys, the horse's temper was easily provoked by teasing, and Rex immediately fought viciously. Two of the scenario clerks began to scream as they were sure that the cowboys would be hurt. In the final editing of the picture, Forde had to cut the scene as it was "just too real," and he feared irate response from the public. After James saw Rex perform, he admitted to Forde that Rex did fit the role.

Forde and the script writers had written narration scenes for James in the picture which would show James at his drawing board. His narration was to bridge time gaps in the sequences where Smoky matures from foal to yearling and then to full grown.

James was intoxicated the first time he faced the camera.

"We finally had to stop shooting," says Forde. "He talked in a choppy rhythm, like a five-year-old reading from a school book. We assigned a speech coach for him, but still he read poorly. So we set up cue cards for him to read from, but he had difficulty even with this assistance. We knew he had been drinking, but he kept insisting he had not."

Alice, in a final attempt to have him sober for another try, kept him from liquor by pleading with him to stay home one evening. The next morning in the studio, James had somehow managed to talk a studio hand into buying a bottle for him. When Alice came for him in his dressing room, to take him to the shooting stage, the bottle was on his dresser, and he had a foolish grin upon his face. Alice turned and walked out of the room, and out of the studio.

Forde and the producers finally lost any hopes of having James appear in the film as planned, and the final editing of his scenes allowed only a brief appearance in the released prints. Victor Jory, the actor who played Clint, also found little aid or advice from James for character hints. "This was a hopeless task," Jory recounts. "He offered very few suggestions, and if forced to give an opinion of what my character might do or say, he would only nod his head, or say, 'maybe,' or perhaps just say nothing and look at me."

James never was pleased in the way *Smoky* appeared on the screen, although from an audience and critic standpoint, the film and adaptation from the novel were successful. James' attitude was probably very typical of many authors whose original written work is treated differently by the hands of movie makers.

If *Smoky* upset James, *Lone Cowboy* disgusted him entirely. But he had been forewarned that Paramount Studios was basing their story on the book, and tailoring it for Jackie Cooper, then a juvenile star. *Smoky* received favorable reviews, while *Lone Cowboy* was a disappointment to the critics. Both pictures were released nationally in 1934.

Chapter Seventeen

WHEN Alice left the studio she went to their rented house, packed her belongings and immediately returned to Reno. She had resigned herself that James would do what he pleased, and no one could reason with him. He had always displayed an independent turn of mind, and she was now convinced he would drink himself to death and neither advice nor pleading would stop that fateful approach. To stay with him, she also felt, would wreck her own emotional stability.

James remained in Hollywood that fall and made no attempt to correspond with Alice. In December, James went to New York for a brief visit with Scribner's. A lecture tour had been arranged for him, but the past commitments at the studio had squelched its itinerary, and now he made arrangements for the following year. From New York, James went to Tucson, Arizona.

Alice, meanwhile, stayed in Reno unaware of James' location. Fred wrote her, asking for James' whereabouts, but no one, not even Scribner's whom Alice had called, knew where he had gone.

In Tucson, James began another book. He wrote about a third of his idea and then destroyed the manuscript. This was the first time he had ever destroyed anything he had written, or was unable to feel sufficient confidence in what he wrote. February, March and April passed without anyone hearing from

James. On May 3, 1934, Fred received a telegram from James, asking Fred to come and get him since he was ill. Fred made immediate reservations to leave for Arizona, and instructed Dolly to wire Alice that Bill was sick in Tucson. Both Fred and Alice arrived in Tucson within hours of each other. Fred went to the apartment address listed on the telegram, and was informed by an annoyed and irritated landlord that James was hospitalized following a heart reaction. Trouble with the police was also an unsettled matter. James, and an alcoholic woman, had gone on a spree, which finally ended in James' apartment, where they wrecked the furniture and fixtures. The police were called and the woman was eventually run out of town as an undesirable. Fred settled the damages bill with the landlord for $295.

When Alice visited James in the hospital, he was in acute depression, and cared neither to talk nor to see anyone. The doctor advised Alice that his condition was not serious, but his drinking would have to stop. After James recovered sufficiently to be out of bed, Alice had him committed to the Kimball Sanitarium at La Crescenta, California, and she rented an apartment nearby.

While James was recuperating, evidence began to show that his financial affairs were muddled, and that he was nearly broke. What had happened to most of the money he had received from the studios for the sale of his books was a mystery. Fred had received some of those particular assets for the ranch operations, and Attorney Snell was given only enough to renew some of the Indian leases on Rocking R. When James was questioned about the whereabouts of almost $6,000, he admitted spending much of it, and lending some of it to cowboys. While Alice was aware that James did give money away easily, at other times fairly large amounts disappeared which he would not account for to Alice. In retrospect, Alice believes that James sent money to his family in Canada.

Alice had telephoned Whitney Darrow at Scribner's to inform him of James' condition. Whitney came to Billings to confer with George Snell about James' affairs, since James was behind schedule in his writing for which advances from Scribner's had been made. Whitney agreed to advance additional money for James to pay his pressing bills, if James would begin working immediately. And too, James' business affairs with Scribner's were to be handled exclusively through Snell. Whitney came to La Crescenta to discuss the proposed agreement. James concurred with the conditions, and also discussed arrangements for a lecture tour. Whitney made it quite clear, however, that unless James took hold of himself in the next few months and stopped drinking, the tour would be cancelled.

James hardly recalled any of his actions when he was drunk. When Alice told him of his recent escapade with a "girl friend," James replied, "I can't believe it. Where the hell did I get the energy?"

The doctors advised James that he must quit drinking, as he seemed to express some sort of self-hate and anger when he drank. Moreover, James' black-outs — not remembering what he had done — could have serious consequences, and if not to himself, possibly to others.

The black-outs that would overtake James when he drank heavily produced a conflict and twisted the skein of his character. He became nasty and destructive. Dolly remembers a meanness in him that said terrible things to those around him. "He was a different person entirely when he was drunk, and if it weren't because we knew Bill to be gentle and considerate except when he drank, I'm sure Fred would have left him long before he did. When Bill was like that one could hardly believe how tolerant and gentle a man he really was."

The black-outs began in the early thirties, and actor Victor Jory recalls an incident in the beginning stages:

". . . for instance, he would sit and tell me a story dealing with Montana. His conversation would go something like this: 'I decided that I would ride over the northern hills to look for strays. This particular day I was riding a little buckskin named Copper. Well, sir, just as I got above — the — top — of — the — hi — ll . . .

"At this point Mr. James' eyes would close, and as nearly as I could judge he had fallen asleep or had completely shut out the present situation. Perhaps five minutes later he would suddenly open his eyes and would begin to talk again, but on a completely different subject. It might go like this: 'Well sir, it was the biggest auction I ever attended — at least two or three hundred horses . . .'

"This type of conversation occurred twenty or thirty times during our acquaintance while filming *Smoky*."

The strange alchemy that alcohol wrought on James had happened many times with Alice, and it became a repetitious cycle, predictable as much as it seemed to be inevitable when James drank. The doctors consequently had advised Alice to stay with James, since he needed her very much at this point. Alice agreed, at least until James' condition was improved. But her marriage, she felt, could never be the same again. She could not bear the thought of another episode with one of his drinking bouts, which were becoming more frequent. She had experienced a great hurt, and in a letter to George Snell she wrote:

"I . . . realize that liquor was the cause of it all. I did what any woman would do for a man she cared for at the time, but to forget it all and start over again, I find at this time very hard to convince myself that it is my job to stand by him. I feel that he should be alone now and see how he will take it all when he's sober and looking things square in the face. I can't seem to fit myself in his surroundings without mistrusting him and being afraid he will drink again when I'm around him . . ."

Alice was to be chastised for leaving James. At best, her decision is one of those thoughts of the moment, justified or unjustified, which she felt was warranted.

Alice stayed close while James was recuperating, and within a few weeks he was allowed to leave the sanitarium during the day and stay with Alice at her apartment. With amazing recuperative energies that were typical after his drinking sprees, James thrust himself completely into his writing and art. He was working on *Home Ranch* and the second volume of his *Uncle Bill* trilogy. The first *Uncle Bill* story appeared in 1932, and is a tale of a brother and sister from the east who spend their summers on a western ranch and are "edducated" by an oldtimer in the lore of the west. Some years before, James made the promise to Alice that he would write a book for children who always wanted to go west. *Uncle Bill* was a promise kept by James, and its popularity suggested another summer's visit by Kip and Scootie, with the title: *In the Saddle With Uncle Bill.*

James wrote and sketched each day so as to have his books ready for Scribner's by spring, as was agreed. Scribner's advances to James helped him clear away some of his debts, but he still worried about the ranch which had been jeopardized by his heavy money losses the past year. Hopefully, James made efforts to sell another story to the studios, and set aside a reserve fund for the ranch. During the next two months his story ideas were only mildly received by various studio producers. Paramount hinted strong interest but finally, as did other studios, informed him that they were not buying because of a business slump in productions.

In August, James told Alice that he felt well enough to go back to Montana and finish *Home Ranch*. Alice said that she would return to Reno. James wrote Fred and Dolly:

"I wish I was with you all because I'm sure tired of sticking around here, but it had to be so I could straighten things up and get in shape. I'm pretty well okay now but I'm sure weak from taking so much cleaning out medicine. I'm still taking some and seeing the doctor. Alice and me was over to that ranch in Santa Barbara a couple of weeks ago and I could hardly get on a horse. That sure surprised me, but the doctor says I'll come out of that soon as I begin taking enough exercise. It's a wonder to him that I can navigate at all after the ways he's treated me, but he said he had to do it, and he sure did . . .

"The way it looks now, Alice is not coming back with me. I'm coming to the ranch alone. We've been gitting along fine since I got over my nervousness and after effects of the booze I had in my system, but we've agreed that we better stay apart some more, for a few months anyway and till we make double sure that we'd be happy together and for all time. No use fooling around, and we thought we could decide better and have a better chance to think things over while we're apart, while I'm at the ranch and my mind is normal and she's in Reno or somewhere where she can think things over well . . .

"I'm not so ornary anymore now. Alice and me ain't had a scrap since last evening and that wouldn't have happened only that we got our wires crossed. Alice answered the phone when the waitress Fred told me to sort of keep under my wing for him while he was gone called me up and wanted to use my wing again, then a while later a boy friend of Alice's called up and I answered the phone. I could tell by the sound of his voice that I wouldn't like the way his hair was parted and etc. Anyway that's how the one scrap started, but it wasn't so bad. It only lasted about ten hours. Had another little scrap today as a kind of chaser.

"But laying all jokes aside, I'd like to hear from you buzzards, every damn one of you even if it's just a few lines or a finger print on a piece of toilet paper."

BILL.

Chapter Eighteen

JAMES promised that he now had the "booze" out of his system. When he returned to the ranch he immediately set for himself a galloping pace night and day to finish two books with numerous illustrations. Dolly wrote Alice often, and kept her informed on James' health. Dolly felt sure that James was truly curing himself since he hadn't even taken a glass of beer. Alice replied that she hoped Dolly had not misjudged James; but if he were really cured he could be proud that he did it alone and without sympathy or coddling.

After his work-load eased, James wrote Alice an encouraging letter of progress about his health and his new books. Alice's reply began a pleasant exchange of letters.

Snell watched James' progress closely, and informed Whitney Darrow of his marked improvement and apparent sincerity in his desire to reform. On that notification, Whitney started to arrange an extensive lecture tour for James that coming fall and winter.

In a portion of a long and belated letter, James wrote to Burton Twichell in Connecticut expressing the new leaf he had plucked for himself:

"I sure agree with you as to hitting for the land,[1] there's something about having a good hunk of land that makes 'big money'

[1]Twichell's last letter indicated that he was buying a farm.

seem like nothing but a lot of trouble. But I have some money to square up that hunk I have and square up with all my obligations. After that I sure plan on living on my land and from my cattle. Mixing my writing with my riding is my idea of fine and peaceful living, and reaching on and on for big and bigger money wont get no gray hairs in my head."

Tragically, however, the new horizon James had set for himself completely faded when, one afternoon, James came out of his studio drunk.

It happened the very day he had gone to town to mail the final chapter of *Home Ranch* to Scribner's. For the rest of the summer, James brooded about the ranch, or stayed with friends in Billings. Liquor turned him again to near hibernation in his own inner-sanctum.

Fred and Dolly, who had felt helpless anguish when they saw James drunk, wrote Alice telling of James' relapse. Alice wrote back that she wasn't surprised, and doubted very much if her presence would have kept James from drinking.

James left the ranch that fall for his scheduled tour in the east. Before going to New York, he went home to Canada for the last time. As told earlier, this visit was one of sad family turmoil, when James insisted that all letters, pictures and drawings identifying him as Ernest Dufault be destroyed.

Alice was living in Reno with her sister, Ann, at the beginning of 1935. She had not heard from James for half a year. Dolly had written to her occasionally, but she too had not heard of James' whereabouts, although he would show up unexpectedly and then disappear again.

Neither Dolly nor Fred offered any advice to James on his conduct. But Fred was deeply worried about the ranch, since it would be lost if James did not get his work to Scribner's. One time, deeply concerned, Fred pointed out to James that his drinking was jeopardizing the ranch, and also killing him. James listened quietly, but finally interrupted Fred by insisting that drinking helped him to concentrate.

When James left again, without notice, he left a note for Fred:

"Your sure a lucky feller," he wrote, "and that's what a feller gets for being good. I could maybe had the same if I'd been good. Dont worry about the ranch ever slipping away, handle it the same as you always did and things will be smooth again, and dont let anybody pester you with bills."

Fred was in a dilemma. He was too fond of James, and had been with him too long to leave him. Nonetheless, he realized that the ranch could not exist unless James earned funds; and he wondered, in spite of James' note, if he were reliable any longer for that responsibility. Fred's wonderment was not long lasting.

James returned about a week later, with a woman. She entrenched herself as James' guardian, and soon began to issue instructions to the cook as to what James should have to eat. She also gave advice to Fred on ranch matters. Fred told her to "go to hell." She suggested that Fred speak to James about their differences. Fred went to James and protested the woman's meddling. James threw his hands in the air with a gesture of non-interference and said, "Well, if that's the way she wants it . . ."

The next day, Fred, Dolly and Clint moved into Billings and, within a week, back to Reno. They were never to see James again.

The *bad things* continued to pile.

During one of James' fully soused sprees, he wrote out a bill of sale for the ranch for $1,000. Alice was quickly notified by her own lawyer in Billings, who advised her to come there as soon as possible.

The bill of sale was partially nullified, although the ranch stock and equipment had been sold by the buyer. Since James might not as easily be spared in the future if he did something similar again, drunk or otherwise, a legal separation was advised for Alice. She was to receive the ranch property, and James was to retain all rights to his published works.[2]

<hr>

[2]An interesting note during the legal proceedings of the above was James' earnings. In 1932 he had earned in excess of $25,000. The previous few years were almost as high in earnings. *James vs. James,* Billings Court House Records.

Chapter Nineteen

BENEATH the surface of human life are the eternal mysteries of human nature. Will James, a modern Ulysses whose own odyssey had shown the gleam of the west to the east . . . became lost himself in a haunting pathos of that past. He followed the wanderlust almost in an endless dream of trying to find the peace and beautiful life rhythm he had enjoyed as a lone cowboy twenty-five years before. All he could find was the echo of his memory. When lost in an alcoholic stupor, his thoughts often came mumbling from his lips about the good old days — when he was just a broke cowboy, free to follow the winds as a sagebrush tumbling along the desert and mountain foothills by the slightest hint of a breeze.

Success had cost James a tragic price. While it had made him a hero, as the public adores heroes, the astuteness of F. Scott Fitzgerald's . . . "show me a hero and I will write you a tragedy" . . . fits with mold-like perfection to Will James. He had lost Alice, Fred, Dolly, and Clint for whom he had planned to do so much; and gone was the Rocking R which was his sentimental dream of the west. Worse, he lost his own self-respect through his fictionalized life, which betrayed both Alice and his family in Canada.

While James was ever aloof to any close friendship, Earl and Eleanor Snook, who conducted an artist's supply house in Billings, became the exception. From the moment James had moved to his ranch in Pryor he had drawn close to the Snooks, and often he would stay at their home in Billings when he had his problems with Alice. Over the years, they provided James with a cellar study for him to work in.

Soon after James' world had shattered beneath him, Earl found out his true identity through some letters to James from his brother Auguste. James swore Earl to lifetime secrecy regarding his true identity.

There was actually little left in Montana to hold James there. He became a drifter again; to New York only when necessary, while Hollywood became his stomping grounds, where he caroused with motion picture cowboys and stuntmen, or followed the rodeo circuit. He never wrote Alice or Fred, and severed all ties with the family he had so frequently proclaimed as the one he had never had.

Yet, there was an amazing tenacity in James to write. Whenever he was sick from the long flooding of his body with alcohol, he returned to the Snooks, and in the basement of their home he wrote and sketched. Earl Snook, meanwhile, had assumed guardianship over James. Whitney Darrow approached Earl to supervise James' responsibilities, as Whitney could no longer depend on James to answer his mail relative to his books and affairs with Scribner's. Whitney worked through Earl to keep James writing, since he had submitted parts of a book, but was then behind with the remaining chapters and illustrations.

Reluctantly, Earl had at times committed James to the hospital, where he was at least forced to sober himself and finish what book he was currently writing.

When James returned to Billings in 1937, he was critically ill, and involved in a car accident. The Billings newspapers reported the story, which was released over a national wire:

COWBOY ARTIST ORDERED TO HOSPITAL
AS ALCOHOLIC

BILLINGS, MONT., (AP) Will James, cowboy artist and author was ordered confined in the Hospital for Inebriates at Warm Springs...by District Judge Guy C. Derry. A jury of physicians found that the 40 (sic) year year old writer ... "is unsafe to be at large in the community due to his excessive drinking, which has affected his mind and health."

Earl's wife, Eleanor, remembers how pitiful it was to visit James, as he would beg for Earl to get him out. Earl could no longer visit and face James' pleading, since he knew the only way to help James was to follow the doctor's advice and hold James at the hospital for his own sake. James even wrote to Whitney, and promised he would go immediately to work if Whitney would influence a discharge for James from the hospital.

By early 1938 he was released. Quiet, sullen and reserved from the rebuffs, James retreated to his basement studio in the Snook home. Immediately he went to work on a book he had been writing during the past year before confinement. It was a rodeo story titled, *Flint Spears,* and based on his article, "How Would You Like to Buck This Game," that was published in *American Magazine* in 1932. He also began working on the third volume of his Uncle Bill trilogy, *Look-See Uncle Bill.*

Earl and Eleanor Snook were able to hold James to Montana for a year. Earl had a ranch which, at that time, was on the outskirts of Billings, on a high bluff overlooking the Yellowstone River. Often James went there to work and ride. He still drank, but fear of confinement again checked him from excessiveness.

In 1939, he left for New York, but returned within a month. There was no particular reason for his trip other than to apparently get away for a time. *The Dark Horse* appeared this same year and the following year, 1940, *Horses I Have Known.* These were the first major horse stories since his *Scorpion, A Good*

Bad Horse was published in 1936. Scorpion wasn't in much competition with his other stories. It was somewhat far-fetched as concerned with the human actors, but Scorpion's incorrigibility throughout the story allowed James some fine story telling between the two bronc busters. They banter words about and discuss the minute traits of Scorpion's bucking habits in the detailed lingo of their profession, all but forgotten today:

"I've got one started," says Pete. "Turned out as gentle as a frozen snake but he thawed out on me."

Unfortunately, James' excellent range terminology and descriptions of Scorpion's very different personality among horses has been forgotten since the rest of the book was unexceptional.

But in a straightforward way, *The Dark Horse* has a credible plot and easy telling. And, *Horses I Have Known* is a series of horse stories, with some excellent writing, of James' experiences with horses. A story or two are a bit questionable, but over-all, they demonstrate James' marvelous understanding of horses. His empathy with them, and his ability to read their behavior by only the slightest reflectional change in their eyes, the way they position their bodies for a certain action, or cock their ears, credit him with an absorbing interest and understanding of horse nature.

James' storytelling in his last years is analyzed with mixed opinions by most reviewers. But his illustrating was definitely deteriorating. Whitney Darrow wrote to Earl Snook of Scribner's concern:

"... Bill's illustrations were terrible ... there is a feeling that he may not be able to come back in his illustrating. A book without his own illustrations would not amount to anything ..."

In the meantime, James had been accused by critics of being "washed up" because of his matrimonial troubles and his "illness." To the former James replied, "... If I knew women like I knew horses all my troubles would be over." And his illness he dismissed by saying . . . "I've always had a certain amount of work to do. I have done it. I'm going to keep on doing it in spite of hell and damnation."[1]

James held to his oath, and with amazing resiliency he sprang above the hell and damnation. He would tear loose with Death Valley Scotty in Hollywood, or with rodeo contestants in Calgary, Madison Square Garden, Cheyenne. But he always returned to Billings to write.

For many years James had always believed that the great American novel would be written with a setting in the west. For only in the west, he felt, was there the strength for character study and setting to justify what was uniquely American in spirit. He even hinted that he might be the one to write the epic. Maybe James was boasting at the time, or playing with the news press. Nevertheless, he had an idea he fostered as a bid to that singular achievement. It had swum in his mind for five years, and he called his story, *The Saga of The American Cowboy,* a sweeping chronicle of the cowboy told through three generations of westerners. Starting with the Texas trail drivers herding the cows through natural grass wilderness, the story evolved to the cowboy at the turn of the century and the devastation that wire fences brought to their lives. The range was closed and with it a way of life. "Too bad," had said James, " . . . It was a good way . . ." Finally, the heritage of the man on horseback was to be continued in the rider of the 1940s . . . three generations of riders, and each named Bill. Each a man of specific energies that molded his own way of life in a western range tradition. Moreover, James wanted to show, graphically, that the cowboy was not a man as is made in the east and who was only an extension of British and European social customs. James' cowboys could not imitate the east, for only men of stagnant energy imitate, and James' three gen-

[1]*Billings Gazette,* January 13, 1935.

erations of cowboys were to be men who stood high in their saddles and in a country ... "where there's mountains and badlands that no dam and irrigation will ever be able to take away from the cowboy, just as free and open as it ever was and will ever be that way ..."

The idea James had discussed with an agent in Hollywood, who in turn had interested MGM Studios in a treatment of the story for motion picture possibilities. In 1940 the agent informed James of the studio's interest. James accepted a contract to write a preliminary treatment of the idea, and went to Hollywood. Almost immediately, procrastination edged his determination to write. Studio deadlines for phases of the story were met by James only through considerable urging by his agent. Periodically, James disappeared — no one knew where — but invariably returned with apologies, and promises to finish the story. By 1941, studio officials finally abandoned the project, and James began turning his story into a book. Dick Dickson, who in association with Harry Sherman was producing pictures at the time, discussed with James a willingness to buy the film rights to his story once it was finished. To help speed the writing of the book, Dickson invited James to stay at Dickson's ranch in Palm Springs. There, in late 1941, James completed writing his *Saga of the American Cowboy*. He moved back to Hollywood, and rented a house, where for the winter he would sketch the illustrations. By then, James had changed the book's title to *The American Cowboy*. The illustrations arrived sporadically at the Scribner's office. Whitney Darrow became annoyed at the delays by James, and asked Earl Snook to go to Hollywood and give James a push. The best Earl could do was press James to promises in finishing what he had started. Whitney had also instructed Earl to tell James that Scribner's could not allow any more advances, and that the only way James could get money from them was to have them sell books. And to sell books, James had to write them.

Alice came to Hollywood that summer, and through a studio agent, obtained James' Irving Avenue address. She had not seen or heard from him in six years. As long as she was in Hollywood, she felt, it was proper for her to stop by and say hello. Alice was met at the door by a woman, who announced herself as James' secretary, and showed Alice into the living room. Five minutes later, James appeared, neither cordial nor indignant. Alice was shocked at his appearance. He was thin, and his cheeks were puffed. He made no effort to promote a conversation, and never asked about Alice's mother, Fred, Dolly or Clint. He spoke about his latest book, and that it was to be made into a motion picture. Alice could not believe he was the same man she had known. It was as if she were staring at a stranger, who had no recollection of a past life with her. She became uneasy, and forced an excuse to leave. James only raised his hand to her for a goodbye.

By July James was entirely finished with *American Cowboy,* and Dickson tried to urge him to return to the Palm Springs ranch to work on a scenario.

"It was hopeless," said Dickson. "For the past year he had been living on liquor. He wouldn't eat. It was difficult to communicate with him."

James was worn and tired after he completed *American Cowboy.* It had sapped even those energies that had always brought on his recuperations. And the hopes that *American Cowboy* would be his best work had fallen dismally below what his mind had imagined. He bemoaned to Dickson that he had spoiled what could have been a great story.

On August 28, 1942, James collapsed in his home, and was rushed to the Hollywood Presbyterian Hospital. He died on September 3 at the age of fifty, from alcoholic complications.

His last will had specified that he be cremated, and that his ashes be scattered over his ranch. Earl Snook came to Hollywood to arrange for the final rites. Alice left for Hollywood immediately after hearing on the radio that James had died.

A ceremony was held at Forest Lawn in Hollywood. A small gathering of acquaintances paid their last respects to James, as the King's Men singing group sang, *Home On The Range*. After the ceremony, Earl returned to Billings with James' ashes.

At two o'clock in the afternoon on September 23, a gathering of friends assembled at James' rimrock studio ranch and while an eulogy was read, James' ashes were scattered from a plane.

The lone cowboy, whose self-advice was to "ride for the high points," both won and lost in a strange pattern of human life.

Afterword

SOME definite items about Will James have been left unsaid because I was unable to prove these stories of him. Also, certain individuals are still alive (and left unmentioned in this book), and the particular weight of these items would be embarrassing to them. Besides, all they really contribute is added fixtures on the already tragic last years of James.

This writer has also avoided any deep and searching judgments of James' relations with other people. What has thus far been told is based on or repeated from interviews by the author. While a biography for perspective and balance may require this analysis, too often the failings of this attempt are apparent when there is concentrated in that beam of attention an over-playing of the sensational and incongruous traits of the individual. Incongruity is a make-up of all people, but the famous and the creative are marked for these idiosyncrasies. Besides, it is only when one acquires a small amount of knowledge for judging others that he also realizes how little he truly knows for making sound judgments — simply because the incongruous suddenly pops up in the individual. All of which brings my thoughts immediately back to James. He was complex, and held many secrets and guilts. His life, as his writings, is a mixture of truth and fiction, of aspirations and frustrations, of deep moodiness, and wild burstings of temperament. If these have complicated the writing of this book, they certainly complicated his relations with other people, as they in turn complicated his.

Nonetheless — yes, I contradict myself — having had the opportunity to claw my way through the hardened shell with which James had fortified himself, I can make some observations that have been neglected by others.

In the years following James' death, his personality and his work have been criticized to extremes, which are detrimental to fairness. Criticisms of him personally have labeled James a phony and an alcoholic. These charges are quite true. They are also the calamitous side of James. What has been overlooked, simply because it was less conspicuous, is that he was also a poignant individual, and made so by a devoted love of the western lands. More than anything else, he humbled himself to a country where "a man can look farther and see less . . . of anything but land and sky." James was never religious, or spoke about religion, but spacial and temporal domain had the feeling of God for him. At times he could turn his mind inward, almost maudlinly, when he saw the country being torn up for farms, homes and roads, and he would reflect a shadowy sense of impatience and inability to do anything about it.

Such a mind delights in reverie, and James delighted in reverie about the open range days, when he rode the country from Canada to Mexico to . . . "no place in particular — just drifting . . . ," and on a good horse that he considered his "fifty-fifty partner," along with a pack horse that carried his home and his grub. Even as James was leading just a vestige of this way of life, progress was pulling out its few remainders from under him.

These thoughts of open range days and drifting only by the compass of his whim were, most likely, dreams that filled James' mind as a boy in Canada. And his thoughts were long thoughts, as a painting fixed on a canvas. Reverie was both an inspiration to write, and a mental retreat for James. The Rocking R — static, peaceful, isolated — was an escape for him, where he could sit on the high bluffs and stare out into the *big sky country*. Only the Snooks were aware how the loss of the ranch to James had wrung him inside.

He found a deep meaning in the land, an experience that he could never completely express in words. In a way, this is the real tragedy of Will James. He does come through in his stories now and then with that feeling of his intense devotion, but not frequently enough. Perhaps if in his later years he had concentrated on quality instead of quantity, he might have left writings of his time and place as memorable as Garland's *Boy Life On The Prairie*.

However, James is not to be ignored for what he does express about the western landscape and cowboys, critters, cattle, horses and stockmen. And in this area, we reach a judgment of James that cannot be ignored; his talents which were offered to the public.

James' writings and style have been discussed, and suffice to say here, *Cowboys North and South*, *Smoky*, *Lone Cowboy*, *All In A Day's Riding* and particular selections from *Drifting Cowboy*, *Sun Up* and *Cow Country* rank high in themes of the west. They were written without excessive frills, and in a language refreshingly unaffected by formality or affectation. These writings have enough realism to be true as the earth itself, and enough touch of romanticism to allow expressions of his soul. The balance is refreshing. His other works, while pleasant to read, are not much more than that, and these include the bulk of his writings.

As an illustrator, particularly of the horse, James is supreme. The horse, as the land itself, was always a surging emotion for him and, unlike his feelings for the land, he could express the power, symmetry and beauty of the horse. By a gleam in its eye, position of an ear, or the dilation of the nostrils, James vividly showed a horse's fear, rage, alertness and, no less powerful, a horse in peaceful repose. A horse could not contort itself into any position that James was unable to photograph in his mind and reproduce that image on paper. Whether in pen and ink, brush and ink, stump and charcoal, or in oils, James' talent breathed life into his horses with an accurate flow of lines. His ease and spontaneity in drawing were a great gift, and as the critics have noted: "For perfect expression of muscle packed energy, James' broncs are inimitable..." "His horses seem to leap from the page and kick dirt all over you..."

James was at his best with pen and ink, and his sketches are evocations of feeling and beauty. But he could become lost with oils. Charles Twichell (son of Burton Twichell) mentions in a letter to the author that a Yale art instructor states James' oils lacked in knowledge of design and composition. Specifically, the instructor pointed to the oil of the three horses fighting, from *Smoky.* "In the right foreground, flying away from the action, is a large jackrabbit which draws as much attention as the horses."

James, unlike the critic, was more concerned with an idea than a rule, and the critic could have selected another of James' oils to substantiate his opinion. The above oil has too much suggestive power of movement in the main horse action to draw away that attention. While some artistic illiteracy is evident in James' composition and design, it is hardly distracting. It is of not much consequence how James expresses himself in his art, so long as the idea fully conveys his feelings. But James cannot stand in the same plateau as Russell or Remington, who lately have been used for unfair comparison. James, after all, was an illustrator — a very graphic illustrator. Russell and Remington were artists. Artists can illustrate, but illustrators cannot necessarily be artists. And while James did not handle his oils in the grander scale as did Russell and Remington, they were more than adequate for what James intended them. In this sense, James' art is highly personal in style, technique and meaning.

And in spite of some critics claim that illustrative works are not worthy of aesthetic considerations, James' illustrations, for the most part, can stand alone. As such, any comparisons with other artists remains only a shallow judgment.

Still, critics and western artists toss about the idea as to whether or not James could have been a great painter. Perhaps he could have been. He did try, and possibly would have relished recognition as an artist more than as a writer. Maybe success and commercialism, family problems, and his own guilts did build to a checkmate and cheat James and his public of his better talents in oils. Maybe too, it was not all James' undoing. In any case one has only his small output of oils with which to gauge whether or not he could have shown a brand of genius equal to Russell and Remington. The question is academic at best, but a certain thought of Dr. Samuel Johnson offers a form of evidence:

"A man of genius has been seldom ruined but by himself."

To Ed Springer –

Here's hoping your lucky star packs
horns – that your rope is tied hard
and your slack is put away –

WILL JAMES
'30

FLY LEAF SKETCH
In gift book sent to Ed Springer in New Mexico.
— *Courtesy of Ed Springer.*

Sources, Acknowledgments

If it were not for an error that Will James entered into his last will and testament, this book probably would not have been written. In paragraph five of his will, James bequeaths part of his estate . . .

"unto Ernest DuFault . . . Ontario, Canada, he being the sole heir and survivor of my dear old friend, Old Beaupre,* who raised me and acted as a father to me . . ."

As I was to learn, James entered his own name on his will. The court could not act upon this paragraph of James' will without first finding Ernest Dufault who, technically, no longer existed. By depositions from Canada, Auguste was forced to relate and prove that Ernest and Will James were the same persons and that obviously, James had meant to say, Auguste. One point is certain; even in death James wanted to hide his true identity. Only through a slight chance, while going through the courthouse records in Billings, did this writer come upon the depositions.

Earl Snook became involved in the estate dispute, and through him did Alice first learn of the actual identity of her husband. In addition to Alice, the Snooks, the Conradts, and a few others legally involved, James' real identity was held secret by them until now.

*Bopy.

The passing years have, however, made less urgent the requirements for secrecy. And too, history must correct itself in the long run.

In addition to the depositions of Auguste Dufault and his letters to this writer, James' prison record at the State Prison in Carson City,† the Ely *Times,* previously footnoted, and particularly the many letters and private papers of James now in the possession of Eleanor Snook of Billings, have been instrumental for this story on James. The newspaper files on James in the Parmly Billings Library are a record of his ranch and local events involving James. Most of the items listed in section seven of the bibliography were of little value, since they tended to play up James' story of being an orphan, and with Bopy. Nonetheless, a little item now and then was helpful.

Footnoting has been slight throughout the text, and used only when the items were available. Otherwise, it is to the following persons I express a deep and sincere gratitude. Each knew James mostly by the prints he had made while they were with him. Whence he came and where he went, his tracks were silently threaded. But each of these persons has helped connect for me the long trail — and the short side trails — that James made:

Especially to Dolly Conradt of Reno for letters, pictures, and her recollections, which helped immensely toward establishing the continuity of James' life. Especially too, to Bob Robertson of Carson City, whose quick mind, backed by sound perspective, often helped me out of quandaries I habitually slipped into during the writing. To him also, I owe many of the leads to people and sources that proved so beneficial. Also to Jeff Rice, Winnemucca; Mrs. James Riordan,* Carson City; Pete Peterson, Tonapah; Charles Keough,* Tonopah; Jane Atwater, Carson City;

*Deceased.

†Now transferred to Special Collections Dept., University of Nevada Library.

Mrs. Emery King, Fallon; Fred Jackson, Tonopah; Jack Connolly, and Mr. and Mrs. Ed Slavin, also of Tonopah. And to Alice James (Mrs. John Ross), Lake Tahoe, for the letters, notes and the many hours she cheerfully granted me both in her home and through correspondence.

Also to:

Curly Eagles,* Van Nuys, California; Clarence Jones,* North Hollywood; Victor Jory, Hollywood; Dick Dickson,* Palm Springs; Lee Rice, San Leandro; Eugene Forde,* Hollywood; Joe De Yong, Hollywood. Ben Steele, Bill Hagen, and George Snell, all of Billings. Also, Ed Springer* of Cimarron, New Mexico for letters and pictures; Ed Blackmore, Grand Junction, Colorado; Lloyd Garrison, Dawson Creek, British Columbia; Charles Twichell, New Haven, Connecticut, for releasing to me correspondence between his father (Burton Twichell) and Will James; and Ross Santee.*

And to the following people, my thanks for their interest in my interest . . .

Dorothy Reading, Carmel, California; Mary Roderick, Carson City, Nevada; former Warden Jack Fogliani, Nevada State Prison, Carson City; Lillia Pepper, Albert and Nell Laird, Carson City, Nevada; Parish of St. Nazaire de Acton, Quebec, Canada; General Services Administration, St. Louis; 20th Century Fox Studios, Hollywood; *Sunset Magazine*, Menlo Park, California; Jerry Armstrong, *Western Horseman*, Colorado Springs, Colorado; Barbara Maseuth, Nevada State Library; and Stanley Adams, formerly director of Readers Services of the Nevada State Library, for his suggestions, criticisms and valuable reference assistance; and Nancy Bowers, also of the Nevada State Library, who arranged so many inter-library loans for me.

*Deceased.

Bibliography

I — Books

Cowboys, North and South. Scribner, 1924

Story Collection from —

Scribner's Magazine

Cowboys, North and South (Dec. 1923).
Bucking Horses and Bucking-Horse Riders
(Mar. 1923).
A Cowpuncher Speaks (Apr. 1923).
Cattle Rustlers (Aug. 1923).
Winter Months in a Cow Camp (Feb. 1924).
Makings of a Cow-Horse (Apr. 1924).
The Longhorns (June 1924).

Saturday Evening Post

Piñon and the Wild Ones (May 19, 1923).

The Drifting Cowboy. Scribner, 1925.

Story collection from —

Sunset Magazine

Desert Range Riding (Dec. 1923).
When Wages Are Low (June 1925).
First Money (Feb. 1925).

THE DRIFTING COWBOY *(continued) —*

> *Saturday Evening Post*
> > Once A Cowboy (June 7, 1924).

> *Southwest Review*
> > Filling in the Cracks (July 1925).

> *Consolidated Magazines Corporation*
> > A Cowboy in the Making.
> > His Waterloo.

> Translated into Swedish, 1929.

*SMOKY, THE COWHORSE. Scribner, 1926.

> Published in serial form in *Scribner's Magazine,*
> > April-July 1926.

> Scribner's Illustrated Classics edition published 1929.
> Translated:
> > Danish, 1928.
> > Russian, 1928.
> > Japanese, 1954.
> > Yugoslavian, 1957.
> > Swedish, 1959
> > Dutch, 1959.

COW COUNTRY. Scribner, 1927.

> Story collection from —

> > *Saturday Evening Post*
> > > The Wild Horse (Sept. 4, 1926).

> > *Sunset Magazine*
> > > The Last Catch (appeared as The Last Catch at
> > > Sand Wash) (Sept. 1926).

*Filmed as a motion picture in 1934, 1946, 1966.

Cow Country *(continued)* —

> Scribner's Magazine
>> Two Old-Timers (Sept. 1927).
>
> *Consolidated Magazines Corporation* (magazines and dates not located)
>> When In Rome —
>> Monty of the "Y" Bench (A sequel to When In Rome).
>> Silver Mounted.
>> Complete.
>> The Breed of 'Em.

*Sand. Scribner, 1929.

> Abridged in *Triple Western*, Dec. 1949.
> Braille, Clovernook Printing House for the Blind, 1948.

†Lone Cowboy: My Life Story. Scribner, 1930.

> Scribner's Illustrated Classics edition issued in 1932.
> Offered in 15 illustrated Sunday supplements by Bell Syndicate, Inc., New York, N.Y. in 1930.
> Translated into Danish, 1932.
> In Braille, 1939. American Red Cross, Cleveland.
> Talking Book, Cleveland Public Library, 12 records.

Big-Enough. Scribner, 1931.

> Selected chapters appeared in *Blue Book Magazine,* Oct. 1931.

Sun Up; Tales of the Cow Camps. Scribner, 1931.

> Story collection from —
>> Scribner's Magazine
>>> The Making of a Cow-Horse (Apr. 1924).

*Filmed as a motion picture, 1948.
†Filmed as a motion picture, 1934.

SUN UP; TALES OF THE COW CAMPS. *(continued)* —

> Bucking Horses and Bucking-Horse Riders
> (Mar. 1923).
> Cattle Rustlers (Aug. 1923).
> The Young Cowboy (Jan. 1927).
> Jake Adams, Sourdough (Dec. 1929).

> *Sunset Magazine*
> First Money (Feb. 1925).
> The Last Catch ... (Sept. 1926).

> *Southwest Review*
> Filling in the Cracks (July 1925).

> *Consolidated Magazine Corporation; Perry Mason Company* (magazines and dates not located)
> His Spurs.
> On The Dodge.
> Midnight.
> His Waterloo.
> A Home Guard.
> Cupid, the Mustang.
> When In Rome —

UNCLE BILL, A TALE OF TWO KIDS AND A COWBOY, Scribner, 1932.

ALL IN THE DAY'S RIDING, Scribner, 1933.

> Story collection from —

> *Saturday Evening Post*
> Why the High Heels? (Feb. 26, 1927).
> The Round-Up Wagon (July 23, 1927).
> On Circle (Nov. 12, 1927).
> Remuda (Nov. 19, 1927).
> Thirty Years' Gathering (Apr. 7, 1928).

ALL IN THE DAY'S RIDING *(continued)* —

> The Big Hat (Sept. 1, 1928).
> Hooks (Dec. 15, 1928).

> *Scribner's Magazine*
> Wound Up (May 1927).
> Down The Wash (Nov. 1927).
> Once When the Laugh Was on Me (Mar. 1928).
> Up in the Eagle Territory (June 1928).
> One That Won (June 1929).
> The Turning Point (Aug. 1929).
> A Stampeder (Feb. 1930).

> (Original sources not located)
> Range Table Etiquette.
> The Cowboy Today.
> A Cowboy to Be.
> Range Blacksmith.
> The Old Slicker.
> The Critter.
> On the Drift.
> Horseflesh.

THE THREE MUSTANGEERS. Scribner, 1933.

IN THE SADDLE WITH UNCLE BILL. Scribner, 1935.

YOUNG COWBOY. Scribner, 1935.
> Arranged from *Big Enough* and *Sun Up*.

HOME RANCH. Scribner, 1935.

SCORPION, A GOOD BAD HORSE. Scribner, 1936.

COWBOY IN THE MAKING. Scribner, 1937.
> Arranged from first chapters of *Lone Cowboy*.

LOOK-SEE WITH UNCLE BILL. Scribner, 1938,

THE WILL JAMES COWBOY BOOK, edited Alice Dalgleish. Scribner, 1938.

> Contains selections from *Lone Cowboy, Uncle Bill, All In A Day's Riding*.

FLINT SPEARS, COWBOY RODEO CONTESTANT. Scribner, 1938.

> Story first appeared in *American Magazine*, June 1932 under the title, "How Would You Like To Buck This Game."
> Braille; Braille Institute of America, Los Angeles, 1940.

THE DARK HORSE. Scribner, 1939.
> Braille; Braille Institute of America, Los Angeles, 1940.

HORSES I'VE KNOWN. Scribner, 1940.

MY FIRST HORSE. Scribner, 1940.

THE AMERICAN COWBOY. Scribner, 1942.

WILL JAMES BOOK OF COWBOY STORIES. Scribner, 1951.
> Foreword by Ross Santee.

II — BOOK INTRODUCTIONS WRITTEN BY WILL JAMES

FRENCH HEELS TO SPURS, by Loraine H. Fielding. The Century Co., 1930.

III — BOOK REVIEWS WRITTEN BY WILL JAMES

In: *Bookman*, Aug. 1928, in review column, "Far West, Near West."

Buckeroo, a story of Piñon Ranch, by Fjeril Hess, Macmillan Co., 1931, in *Saturday Review of Literature*, Sept. 19, 1931.

IV — WILL JAMES STORIES CONTAINED IN ANTHOLOGIES

BRONC TWISTER STEPS UP
  Hogeboom, Amy. *Boys' Book Of The West*. Lothrop, 1946.

BUCKING HORSES AND RIDERS
  Rice, Grantland and Harford Powell. *The Omnibus of Sports*. Harper, 1950.

CHAPO — THE FAKER
  Dennis, Wesley. *Palomino and Other Stories*. World, 1956.

A COWBOY AND HIS PONY
  Junior Classics, Vol. 7. *The Animal Book*. Collier & Son, Corp., 1938.

FIRST MONEY
  Self, Margaret C. *Treasury of Horse Stories*. Barnes, 1945.

GOOD-BY, SMOKY
  Cavanah & Weir. *24 Horses*. Rand & McNally Co., 1950.

HIS FIRST BRONC
  Gruenberg, Sidonie. *Favorite Stories Old And New*. Doubleday, 1955.

HIS SPURS
  Fenner, Phyllis, *Cowboys, Cowboys, Cowboys*. Watts, F., 1950.

LAST CATCH . . .
  Coleman, Rufus A. *Western Prose And Poetry*. Harper, 1932.

LAST CATCH AT SAND WASH
  Clarke, Frances. *Gallant Horses*. Macmillan, 1954.

LONE COWBOY
  Fenner, Phyllis. *Cowboys, Cowboys, Cowboys*. Watts, F., 1950.

MIDNIGHT

Fenner, Phyllis. *Cowboys, Cowboys, Cowboys*. Watts, F., 1950.

RIDING BOG

Targ, W. *American West*. World, 1946.

SEEING EYE

Cooper, Page. *Great Horse Stories*. Garden City, 1954.

SEEING EYE

Brown, Beth. *All Horses Go To Heaven*. Grosset & Dunlap, 1963.

SMOKY

Seton, Ernest Thompson, *Famous Animal Stories*. Coward-McCann, 1932.

SMOKY AND OLD TOM

Macauley, T. *Great Horse Omnibus*. Ziff-Davis, 1949.

SMOKY AND THE WOLVES

Harper, Wilhelmina. *Flying Hoofs*. Houghton, 1939.

SMOKY, RANGE COLT

Arbuthnot, May Hill. *Arbuthnot Anthology Of Children's Literature*. Scott, 1953.
———. *Time For True Tales And Almost True*. Scott, 1953.

SQUEAK OF LEATHER

Fenner, Phyllis. *Horses, Horses, Horses*. Watts, F., 1949.

TOM AND JERRY

Kelley, Robert F. *Junior Sports Anthology*. Howell, Soskin, 1945.

V — Individual Drawings Which Appeared in Sunset Magazine

One Man Horse (Jan. 1920).

Mothers (Feb. 1920).

The Leppy (Mar. 1920).

Insult To Injury (Apr. 1920).

Man and His Ways (May 1920).

Was You Looking For Bear . . . (June 1920).

When a Feller Needs a Friend (Aug. 1920).

Playing With Fire (Sept. 1920).

A Friend In Disguise (Oct. 1920).

Keno, the Cowhorse (Nov. 1920).

A Change of Heart (Jan. 1921).

A Chance Reunion (Mar. 1921).

'Twould Make a Feller Think Twice (Apr. 1921).

An Opportune Challenge (May 1921).

The Wrong Party (June 1921).

The Right of Way Without Argument (July 1921).

The Prodigal's Return (Sept. 1921).

When Ignorance Is Bliss (Oct. 1921).

A Privileged Character (June 1924).

Trouble Seldom Comes Singly (July 1924).

Those Who Watch Over Us (Aug. 1924).

VI — ILLUSTRATIONS FOR OTHER AUTHORS*

A. BOOKS

Mills, Enos A. *Watched By Wild Animals*. Doubleday, 1922.
———. *Wild Animal Homesteads*. Doubleday, 1923.

Burns, William Noble. *Tombstone*. Doubleday, Doran, 1929.

McCarthy, Don. ed. *Language of The Mosshorn*. Billings, Gazette Printing Co. 1936.

B. ARTICLES

Walt Coburn's Action Novels (pulp magazine) (circa 1920).

"The Varmint," by E. C. Lincoln. (*Sunset;* Feb. 1920).

"The June Trail," by E. C. Lincoln. (*Sunset;* July 1920).

"Ridin' And Thinkin'," by Jack Burroughs. (*Sunset;* Dec. 1920).

"Visitin'," by E. C. Lincoln (*Sunset,* Jan. 1921).

Action Stories (pulp magazine); covers and inside illustrations (Apr., Oct., 1922, *et al.*)

"The Sheep Killers," by Fred Coleman Sears (*The Youth's Companion;* Oct. 30, 1924).

"The Family Man," by A. M. Van Deusen (*Sunset;* Dec. 1924).

"The Ride That Made Buffalo Bill Famous," by (*Fawcett's Magazine;* 1925).

"Rough's Last Fight," by Billy Dohlman (*Sunset;* May 1925).

"Patsie," by Billy Dohlman (*Sunset;* June 1925).

"King, Son of Gold-Dust," by Billy Dohlman (*Sunset;* Nov. 1925).

*This listing is not to be considered complete.

"Ebenezer's Ride," by W. S. Jennings (*The Youth's Companion;* Nov. 26, 1925).

"More About King," by Billy Dohlman (*Sunset;* Dec. 1925).

"Locoed," by V. Stewart Boyd (*Sunset;* Sept. 1927).

Haven, Story Of A Wild Horse," by Hal Borland. (*Ladies' Home Journal;* Nov. 1927).

The American Boy Magazine; Nov. 1928).

"Dude West," by Mary Roberts Rinehart (*Ladies' Home Journal;* Apr. 1929).

"The Rope And The Bulldog," by Thompson Burtis (*American Boy-Youth's Companion;* June 1930).

VII — BIOGRAPHICAL[*]

ARTICLES AND BOOKS

"A Letter from Will James to Charlie Russell," Los Angeles Westerner's Corral; *Branding Iron*, Dec. 1948.

"Across The Editor's Desk," *Sunset*, Dec. 1924.

Amaral, Anthony. "Will James and the Horse Called Happy," *Western Horseman*, May 1964.

Branch, Douglas. *The Cowboy And His Interpreters*. Appleton, 1926.

"Bucked and Battered to Fame," *American Magazine*, May 1931.

Corley, George. "Will James as I Knew Him," *Rocky Mountain Empire Magazine*, Jan. 5, 1947.

Cormack, Bob. "Will James," *Denver Westerner's Brand Book*, 1962.

[*]This listing is not to be considered complete.

"Editorial Comments," *The Lariat*, Mar. 1924.

"Editorial Comments," *Triple-X Western Stories*, Nov. 1925.

Editor to Author; The Letters of Maxwell E. Perkins, Charles Scribner's Sons, 1950.

Flack, M. "Will James at Home," *Wilson Bulletin*, Mar. 1938.

Johnson, M. Comp. "American First Editions," *Publishers Weekly*, Nov. 21, 1931.

"John Newbery Prize Book," *Journal of National Education Association*, Oct. 1927.

Montgomery, E. R. *Story Behind Modern Books*, Dodd.

"Our Family Album," *Ladies' Home Journal*, Nov. 1927.

"Portrait," *Publishers Weekly*, April 13, 1935.

"Portrait," *Sunset*, Aug. 1926.

Scully, Frank. *Armour Bright*. Chilton, 1963.

"Self Portrait," *Arts and Decorations*, Oct. 1930.

60 Years of Best Sellers – 1895-1955. Alice Payne Hackett, R. R. Bowker, Co., 1956.

"Smoky, John Newbery Prize Book," *National Education Association Journal*, Oct. 1927.

"Spirit of Will James," *Western Livestock Journal*, Feb. 15, 1943.

"Will James – A Young Old-Timer," *The Rider and Driver*, Feb. 6, 1926.

Wilson, B. V. "A Heap More Than Words," *Western Horseman*, Sept. 1952.

What should be an informative source is the James-Scribner correspondence file. This writer made an attempt, in person, at the Scribner Building in New York, for permission to examine the James file. I was told that the file was in a storehouse and could not be made available.

While this book was in its page proofs, *Publisher's Weekly* reported that the Princeton University Library had been chosen as the depository for the Scribner archives. The letters of Will James are included and, presumably, will be available for researchers.

Index

BOOKS OF THE WEST . . . FROM THE WEST